"Hugh Whelchel has done an exquisite job of calling Christians to their role in the kingdom of God. He is straightforward in his approach and direct in stating his own opinion. At the same time he weaves the thoughts of many, many others from Calvin to Keller into the development of this concise book that begins with foundation of Biblical theology and moves all the way to our individual and collective callings as believers in the Almighty God of this universe. It is a must read, wonderful for profound discussions."

Dr. Robert C. Varney
Former hi-tech CEO
Currently VP of the Leader-led Movements for
Global Cities at Campus Crusade for Christ International

This is exactly what the church needs, clear-eyed and even inspiring thinking about work. Somewhere along the way we lost sight of the meaning, even the beauty, of work. Hugh Whelchel helps us view our work as God intended. It was Moses who declared that God in his graciousness will establish the work of our hands—yes, even the mundane, routine, earthy work of our hands. Read this book and you'll find out just how delightful work can be.

Stephen J. Nichols
Research Professor of Christianity & Culture
Lancaster Bible College
Author of *Welcome to the Story: Reading, Loving, and Living God's Word*

"The dignity and goodness of work is a truth taught from the first chapter of Genesis, yet even Christians often miss the richness of the Bible's teaching on the subject. Too often, we imagine that work is a necessary evil that we must endure as a result of man's fall into sin. But even God is described as "working" when He creates the heavens and the earth. And His first blessing to man and woman is to be fruitful and multiply, to have dominion over the earth, to till the garden and keep it. God the Creator has created us to create.

"Plumbing the riches of Scripture and the Reformed tradition, Hugh Whelchel has done a masterful job of reminding us of this biblical picture of work. When we work, we participate in that kingdom to come in which God will create a new heaven and a new earth."

Jay W. Richards, Ph.D.
Author of *Money, Greed, and God*, Co-author of *Indivisible*, and Executive Producer of *The Call of the Entrepreneur*

"Hugh Whelchel's *Rediscovering the Biblical Doctrine of Work* is a wonderful contribution to the current discussion of vocation, work, church and culture. It is short, pointed, concise, clear, well-documented. It is the perfect antidote to ideas held by many that the Kingdom of God is to be found only in the institutional church. It motivates us to treat our labors as God's calling and to do all things to his glory. Everybody should read it."

Dr. John Frame
Professor of Systematic Theology and Philosophy
Reformed Theological Seminary Orlando

"This is a Biblically-based and compelling argument supporting the integration of faith and work into a noble calling to serve God in the marketplace."

Steve Reinemund, Dean of Business,
Wake Forest University Schools of Business
Retired Chairman and CEO, PepsiCo

"Our vocation: Curse or obsession? In *How Then Should We Work*, Hugh Whelchel begins with first principles and lays out the Biblical case that our work is neither a necessary evil nor the center of our self-worth. Rather, it is God's holy calling through which we use our God given talents for the furtherance of His ultimate plan—the Kingdom of God. A compelling read, highly recommended."

Hon. John Scott Redd, Vice Admiral, U.S. Navy (Ret.)
First Director of the U. S. National Counterterrorism Center
Founding Commander of the U. S. Navy's 5th Fleet in the Middle East

"My father was a 'layman', but he accomplished more for the Kingdom of Christ than I have done as a minister and the chancellor of a seminary. This excellent book by Hugh Whelchel will help you see all that you do, especially your 'work' as a calling from God and as a place of opportunity and responsibility to serve Christ."

Robert C. (Ric) Cannada, Jr
Chancellor and CEO Reformed Theological Seminary

"What an important book! We often sing, 'I owe, I owe, I owe and it's off to work I go.' That's from the pit of hell and smells like smoke and Hugh Whelchel will tell you why in this book. Not only does he do that, he does it in a refreshing way with great Biblical insight. When you add the wisdom of his lifetime of experience to the mix, you have a book that ought to be read by every Christian, underlined and referenced often and then given to everybody you know. You will 'rise up and call me blessed' for having commended this book to you and Hugh Whelchel for having written it."

Steve Brown
Key Life Ministries
Author of *Three Free Sins: God Isn't Mad at You*

"From the time of Adam and Eve, when they were gardeners, to Abraham tending sheep to Jesus working in his father's carpentry shop, work is Biblical. Often there's a disconnect in integrating work with our mission and purpose. Hugh's book tackles that issue head on—well worth your time if you want to make Monday through Friday count as much as Saturday and Sunday!"

J.C. Watts, Former Congressman
Author, businessman, preacher and speaker

"Most of our time is spent at work, but even Christians have little understanding of the real purpose of work and its relation to their faith. In this lively book, Hugh Whelchel uses Biblical wisdom, history, and sound logic to help each of us better understand work and its relationship to God's plan for our life. Moreover, as we apply the teachings to our personal lives, we have the opportunity to alter the culture of the 21st century for the better."

James Gwartney,
Professor of Economics, Florida State University
Author of *Common Sense Economics: What Everyone Should Know About Wealth and Prosperity*

"No one has thought more deeply or written more clearly than Hugh Whelchel about the Biblical doctrine of work. In God's economy, Whelchel explains in *How Then Should We Work*, the Christian works, not merely to survive, but to thrive and to flourish for the glory of God, the advancement of the Kingdom, the renewal of the culture, and the benefit of all humankind. The believer's vocational calling is a celebration of the Creator and an act of worship. *How Then Should We Work?* is indispensable reading for Christians who seek a Biblical understanding of vocational calling and desire their work to be a Christian witness."

Daniel L. Dreisbach, Professor of Justice,
Law and Society, American University
Author of *Thomas Jefferson and the Wall of Separation Between Church and State*

"Hugh Whelchel's work comes at a critical time when both the church and the culture in general are questioning the purpose and value of work. His solid examination of the Biblical teaching on work is an excellent starting point for anyone wrestling with these issues. Carefully exploring the Scripture's view of work as an integral part of our calling, he lays out a compelling alternative to the disintegrated and disjointed view of work that is prevalent today. I highly recommend it."

J. Michael Thigpen
Executive Director of the Evangelical Theological Society

"'Our Christian calling finds no separation between the secular and the sacred.' Hugh Whelchel has succinctly identified this core issue each person, including me, yearns to understand. This tangible mystery, that the often mundane, tedious work of our lives is our holy devotion to the creative, dynamic God is profound. Today, you and I are living the call God has on our lives. I have been inspired to invest the capital God has invested in me. I believe you will be inspired as well after reading the Biblical exhortation Hugh lays out in this well-written book."

Jimmy Kemp
President
Jack Kemp Foundation

"Monday morning would have a better reputation if we took to heart Hugh Whelchel's teaching about a Biblical doctrine of work. The work-week would have a deeper sense of purpose, marked by peace and joy rather than anxiety and tension: peace produced from a clearer understanding of the integration of faith and work, and joy from the satisfaction of pursuing our callings to the glory of God and for the shalom of the city in which he's placed us."

Jennifer A. Marshall, Director
Richard and Helen DeVos Center for
Religion and Civil Society at The Heritage Foundation
Author of *Now and Not Yet: Making Sense
of Single Life in the 21st Century*

"*How Then Should We Work?* is as excellent book that calls us to cultivate a Biblical view of work and vocation. Hugh Whelchel provides a wealth of content in readable prose, placing the issue of work squarely within the context of the cultural mandate and the Kingdom of Christ. Additionally the reader gleans many practical insights relevant to serving Christ in the work place. Anyone desiring to rediscover the Biblical doctrine of work should start here."

Shawn Ritenour
Professor of Economics, Grove City College
Author of *Foundations of Economics: A Christian View*

HOW THEN
SHOULD
WE WORK?

REDISCOVERING THE BIBLICAL DOCTRINE OF WORK

HUGH WHELCHEL

WESTBOW
PRESS
A DIVISION OF THOMAS NELSON

Unless otherwise indicated, all Scripture quotations are from The Holy Bible, New International Version®, NIV® Copyright © 1973, 1978, 1984, 2011 by Biblica, Inc.™ Used by permission. All rights reserved worldwide.

Scripture quotations marked (ESV) are from The Holy Bible, English Standard Version® (ESV®), copyright © 2001 by Crossway, a publishing ministry of Good News Publishers. Used by permission. All rights reserved.

Scripture quotation marked (NASB) are from the New American Standard Bible®, Copyright © 1960,1962,1963,1968,1971,1972,1973,19 75,1977,1995 by The Lockman Foundation. Used by permission.

WestBow Press books may be ordered through booksellers or by contacting:

WestBow Press
A Division of Thomas Nelson
1663 Liberty Drive
Bloomington, IN 47403
www.westbowpress.com
1-(866) 928-1240

Because of the dynamic nature of the Internet, any web addresses or links contained in this book may have changed since publication and may no longer be valid. The views expressed in this work are solely those of the author and do not necessarily reflect the views of the publisher, and the publisher hereby disclaims any responsibility for them.

Any people depicted in stock imagery provided by Thinkstock are models, and such images are being used for illustrative purposes only.

Certain stock imagery © Thinkstock.

ISBN: 978-1-4497-4581-3 (sc)
ISBN: 978-1-4497-4584-4 (hc)
ISBN: 978-1-4497-4582-0 (e)

Library of Congress Control Number: 2012906161

Printed in the United States of America

WestBow Press rev. date: 05/10/2012

To my mother

Martha Lathers Whelchel

1928-1990

Heigh-ho, heigh-ho, It's off to work we go . . .

—Larry Morey,
The Dwarfs' Marching Song, 1938

Table of Contents

Foreword

By Rev. Dr. Art Lindsley

C.S. Lewis believed that Jesus Christ was the key to unlock the mysteries of life. He wrote, "I believe in Christianity as I believe that the sun has risen, not only because I see it, but because by it I see everything else." There are times, particularly when we are at a crossroads (personally or culturally), when we need to step back and get a bigger vision, a new paradigm, a renewed perspective on the nature of our lives from a Biblical point of view. Lewis also said in The Magician's Nephew: "For what you see and hear depends a good deal on where you are standing; it also depends on what sort of person you are." If you are standing on the top of a mountain, you can see further than if you are in a valley, and what you see and how you see it depends a lot on what you care about and who you are.

Hugh Whelchel has written a book, *How Then Should We Work? Rediscovering the Biblical Doctrine of Work*, that provides an opportunity for discerning people to get a deeper, panoramic, broader perspective, not only on work, but on all of life. We can see our lives through the grand sweep of Scripture, giving us a context to rightly understand our purpose. Nothing is meaningful without a context. Unless we understand the Biblical framework, we will miss much of what it means to live our lives in Christ.

Narrowed Perspective

Many in the Church, according to Hugh, have narrowed the Gospel to two chapters rather than the Biblical four-chapter Gospel. They have focused on personal salvation (as important as that is) and neglected our purpose in creation and our destiny in a new heaven and new earth. They have largely failed to see that Christ's redemption applies not only to personal life, but also to our corporate life in the Church and to the whole cosmos. Redemption leads to the "restoration of all things" (Acts 3:21).

Creativity

For instance, the Great Commission to make disciples of all nations (Matt. 28:18-20) has often been pursued without reference to the Cultural Mandate—to exercise dominion or rulership over the whole creation (Gen. 1:26-28). Francis Schaeffer and J.R.R. Tolkien maintain that this means we are to be "sub-creators." Only God can create something out of nothing, but we are made in the image of God so that we can create something out of something. We can use clay to make a sculpture, wood to make a table or a house, paint to make a mural, a flute to create a song, mold metal to make a tool, make a computer and access an (almost) infinite amount of information. We are made to use our creativity to shape the world around us using the gifts we are given in the work that we do. If we recovered the centrality of creativity as the task for which we were created, it could unleash new energy, vitality, and focus in the Church, impacting every area of our lives. Hugh's book opens our eyes to see a different vantage point on the Gospel and our drive for creativity.

Purpose

Hugh also expounds our "Calling" to be faithful in all areas of life, including our work. Rick Warren wrote the mega-bestseller, The Purpose Driven Life, accenting the idea that it is not about us. Hugh takes this further to show that our chief purpose is to "glorify God and enjoy Him forever" and that means to glorify Him in every area He has called us to pursue. We are called to be faithful to Him in our personal devotion, our marriages, our families, our role in Church, our place as citizens, and in our work. We need to get out of our own self-focus. John F. Kennedy's famous line, "Ask not what your country can do for you; ask what you can do for your country," is rooted, intentionally or not, on this other-centered, Biblical view of calling. Agape love might be defined as the "sacrifice of self in the service of another." When we give our lives to our Lord, He calls us to give our lives for others in all we do. If every believer heard and acted on Hugh's message here, it would revolutionize our culture.

Freedom

Jesus said that, "If you abide in my Word, then you are really disciples of mine; and you will know the truth, and the truth shall make you free" (John 8:31-32). There is nothing more freeing than knowing, in thought and in life, the truth of Scripture. Hugh's book can help free us from a narrowed perspective, unleash creativity, and clarify our calling and purpose in life. This book will also unfold the meaning of the Kingdom of God, the neglected concept of "Common Grace," and the Biblical meaning of success. His goal is to help us to "reweave shalom." Shalom is God's "peace," but a peace that is more than an absence of conflict or war. It means a universal flourishing, a wholeness, a satisfaction going in every direction. In Jeremiah 29:7, God's people are called to "seek the peace [shalom] and prosperity of the city." This is applied to the city that "I have carried you into exile. Pray to the Lord for it because if it prospers, you too will prosper." Another translation (NASB) puts this latter phrase, "in its peace, you will have peace." Hugh emphasizes that the Scriptures' grand narrative goes from the garden to the city. The tree of life in the garden in Genesis 2 is seen again in the Holy City of Revelation 22. God's purpose is the redemption and restoration of all of life and all of culture.

Transforming Culture

Hugh's book in the end is a call to transform all of culture and bring it under the Lordship of Christ. It might be of value here to note that he advocates for cultural change while upholding religious freedom, political freedom, and economic freedom. While these latter themes are not explicitly developed in the book, it is important to note his commitment to these principles.

There is a scene in the first Star Wars movie where the hero's ship jumps into hyperspace to escape the evil force of the Empire. There is a flash of light, a burst of acceleration, and they are in a different place a long distance away. The evangelical Church needs this burst of light, this thrust forward, in order to catch a bigger vision of the Gospel, the place of creativity and calling in our lives, and a call to cultural transformation. While Hugh's book is very well written, it is not light reading. It will repay a careful, thoughtful reading. You will find fireworks going off in your mind, a new vantage point, a larger view, a new paradigm emerging. Read the book carefully and pass it on to all the leaders you know. Preach and teach these ideas so that these Biblical truths might be embedded deeply in the hearts and minds of people and conveyed to the key leaders, cities, ministries and networks that shape our culture.

Preface

The cold, night wind howled across the desert as I crawled into my sleeping bag and gazed up at a brilliant canopy of stars. It was October 1978, and this was our last night on the Sinai Desert. We had spent many days on the Sinai retracing the historical route of Moses and the children of Israel as they traveled from Egypt to the Promised Land. In my mind, I was still thinking about the devotional delivered an hour earlier in a candle-lit grotto by our expedition leader Jamie Buckingham.

He had read out of the twelfth chapter of Old Testament book of Numbers, which in part says, "Now Moses was a very humble man, more humble than anyone else on the face of the earth." I can remember thinking that being called to be a Bedouin shepherd in the Sinai for 40 years would be enough to teach anyone humility, even the son of a Pharaoh. During our time on the Sinai, we met some of the Bedouin who still live an extremely austere life, almost unchanged from the time of Moses. I went to sleep wondering what God would do with my life. I wanted to follow God with all of my heart, but was uncertain how to integrate my Christian faith with what I was doing professionally.

Fast forward 20 years and I still saw vocational calling in much the same light as I had that night on the desert—it was still very disconnected from my faith. I believed our work was primarily a means through which God taught us virtues like humility, honestly and perseverance, as he had done with Moses. And, of course, our vocational work also provided for our physical needs and provided money for God's work in and through His Church, but little else.

Vocationally, I was working in the business world. If you had asked me then to describe the work I was doing that was important to God, I would have told you about my work in the lay leadership of my Church, the adult Sunday School class that I taught, and the work I did with Christian non-profit groups. I secretly envied pastors, missionaries, and others who got to work "full-time" for God. I saw little if no connection between what I did as a businessman and God's Kingdom.

Something was wrong with this picture, but I was not sure what it was. How could it be that what I did during the majority of week, my vocational work, was not that important to God? When I brought up this concern to my pastor and others at church, I found no satisfactory answers. It remained a mystery without any clues. That is when the hand of God's providence intervened.

I had always been interested in theology and decided to take some classes at Reformed Theological Seminary's Orlando campus. In one class I was introduced to the writings of theologian and author Francis Schaeffer. It was amazing that I had been raised in the Presbyterian Church but never been exposed to his writing, which was now reshaping much of what I believed about my place in this world. About the same time, I was given a new book by Chuck Colson called, *How Now Shall We Live?* Interestingly, it was in many ways an updated version of Schaeffer's work. These books led me to authors like Dutch Reformer Abraham Kuyper and eventually back to the Early Reformers including Luther and Calvin. These authors revolutionized the way I looked at life, work, and the Bible and showed me how to bring all things under the Lordship of Christ, especially the work of my vocational calling.

These authors, whose work called down to me over the centuries, taught that the work of my hands mattered to God. They wrote that our work serves three great ends: it glorifies God, it serves the common good, and it furthers the Kingdom of God. That includes everything we do from the most significant project to the most mundane task.

Discovering the Biblical doctrine of work transformed my life. Work for me went from being just a means to an end to having transcendent purpose in and of itself. It wasn't just an avenue simply for sharing my faith (to evangelize) or to create wealth to donate to missions work; it was the very thing through which I could be the salt and light Jesus called me to be. In fact, my vocational work was part of a larger grand story of God I was discovering, a story that started in the Garden of Eden and continues when Jesus returns and establishes the New Heavens and the New Earth. My work as a businessman, or whatever I was to do, had real value and purpose in God's Kingdom.

An understanding that our work matters to God is incredibly fulfilling and freeing. To quote author Dorothy Sayers, "work is not, primarily, a thing one does to live, but the thing one lives to do. It is, or should be, the full expression of the worker's faculties, the thing in which he finds spiritual, mental, and bodily satisfaction, and the medium in which he offers himself to God."

This book has been written as a simple Biblical primer on integrating our faith and our work. It's the journey through which God took me and I pray can be of help to you. I have pulled together Biblical teaching on faith and work from Christians across the centuries, from the Reformers to contemporary writers like Tim

Keller and Cornelius Plantinga, in an attempt to help you understand the difference between work, calling and vocation and how they should be Biblically applied in your daily life.

Maybe you're where I was 20 years ago, struggling to make sense of your vocational life and wondering if it has any value to God. Or maybe you're a pastor or teacher, shepherding those in the workforce and uncertain how to best equip them. May this book be a means for you to rediscover the Biblical doctrine of work and be ignited with a new sense of purpose: through your vocational calling God has given you a powerful tool to change the world!

By rediscovering the Biblical doctrine of work, Christians can radically impact our culture making a positive, sustainable difference in our communities, our cities, our country and our world for the glory of God and His Kingdom.

Hugh Whelchel
McLean, Virginia
March 2012

Acknowledgments

It has been said, "You will be the same person in ten years as you are today except for the people you meet and the books you read." The writing of many authors has helped shape my understanding of the Biblical doctrine of work including Martin Luther, John Calvin, Abraham Kuyper, Francis Schaeffer, Charles Colson, Nancy Pearcey, Tim Keller, Cornelius Plantinga and many others. Several of my professors at RTS have been instrumental in shaping my thoughts as well, including John Frame, Richard Pratt and Miles Van Pelt. I want to thank my editors Sandy and Dale Larson for their help. Also thanks go to my entire staff at the Institute for Faith, Work & Economics, especially Kristin Hansen for her help in editing and marketing the book. Particular thanks go to everyone in my Sunday school class who let me test much of this material on them and all those who reviewed the book. Last, I want to extend great appreciation to my wife, Leslie, for her patience and encouragement without which this project would have never gotten finished.

Hugh Whelchel
March 2012

CHAPTER 1

Introduction

The LORD God took the man and put him in the Garden of Eden
to work it and take care of it.

—Genesis 2:15

The arena was packed with over 5,000 business people attending a one-day motivational conference. They would listen to some of today's greatest inspirational speakers including General Colin Powell, Dick Vitale and Tony Robbins.

One of the speakers asked the assembled business leaders this question: "If you went home tonight and found that a long lost relative had died and left you ten million dollars, would you be at work tomorrow?"

From all over the arena came a resounding "NO!"

The audience's response is no surprise. A recent Gallup poll found that 77% of Americans hate their jobs. Another poll found that Americans hate their jobs more today than in the past 20 years; fewer than half say they are satisfied with their current job.[1] With 50-hour-plus work weeks and long commutes, workers are spending more and more of their lives at work; yet many of them are unfulfilled and frustrated with their jobs.

Even for many Christians, work is often only a means to an end. Many Christians today have bought into the pagan notion that leisure is good and work is bad. They have also been misled by the sacred/secular distinction, which teaches that working in the church is the only "real" fulltime Christian service.

Such an artificial division between sacred and secular has not always prevailed. The Reformers taught that all labor is noble if it is accepted as a calling and performed "as unto the Lord." This truth has slipped dramatically in both today's church and contemporary culture. Paul Helm in his book *The Callings: The Gospel in the World* says that "Work is part of a Christian's calling . . . . this Biblical idea has had a profound influence in Europe and North America since the Reformation but has largely been forgotten, due to the eclipse of the influence of the Christian gospel from national life."[2]

As followers of Christ, we must address our failure to live as His followers in the workplace and to think theologically about how we integrate our faith and our work. We must learn not just to *work to live*, but to *live to work* for the glory of God.

The doctrine of calling has fallen on hard times in the contemporary postmodern world. Even people in the church speak of their "religious preferences" and "spiritual lifestyles" instead of their God-ordained duties, responsibilities, and privileges. All evangelical Christians would acknowledge that all of life is to be lived under the comprehensive Lordship of Christ (Matthew 28:18). Few, however, understand that even in our everyday work, the Scripture teaches no separation between the secular and the sacred. No church-related work or mission is more spiritual than any other profession such as law, business, education, journalism, or politics. All of our actions should be unified in obedience to God and for God's glory (1 Corinthians 10:31; Colossians 3:17).

The Kingdom of God bears on every dimension of life, and agents of the Kingdom serve as salt and light (Matthew 5:13-16) wherever the Spirit leads them. As we Christians live out our worldview in public life, we help reverse the erosion of truth in a number of different ways. In the midst of the fragmentation of postmodern pluralism, Christians should see all things as unified in God's over-arching plan for the universe, summed up in the supremacy of Christ and His full calling on our lives. In this regard Abraham Kuyper, the great Dutch statesman, theologian, and journalist, made the famous statement, "There is not a square inch in the whole domain of our human existence over which Christ, who is sovereign over all, does not cry: 'Mine!'"[3]

Dorothy Sayers wrote extensively about the problem of work in England after the First World War. In light of where we are in the church today, her writing is prophetic:

> In nothing has the Church so lost Her hold on reality as in Her failure to understand and respect the secular vocation. She has allowed work and religion to become separate departments, and is astonished to find that, as a result, the secular work is turned to purely selfish and destructive ends, and that the greater part of the world's intelligent workers have become irreligious, or at least, uninterested in religion. But is it astonishing? How can anyone remain interested in a religion that seems to have no concern with nine tenths of his life? The Church's

approach to an intelligent carpenter is usually confined to exhorting him not to be drunk and disorderly on Sundays. What the Church should be telling him is this: that the very first demand that his religion makes upon him is that he should make good tables.[4]

Michael P. Schutt in his book *Redeeming Law* recalls his own experience as a young Christian lawyer trying to understand how to integrate his faith and his work. "We wanted to be more than Christians muddling through the law. We wanted to be Christian lawyers, our faith integrated with our calling. We found little guidance in the classroom, from our texts, or from practicing lawyers and professors. Or from our pastors and priests."[5]

Our call to be salt and light in the world requires us to understand not only the dominant cultural forces shaping our environment but also how to use both our primary and secondary callings to positively promote God's Kingdom. The church needs to be teaching lawyers, doctors, construction workers, and mothers homeschooling their children how to carry out their vocational calling from a truly Christian perspective.

Carl F. H. Henry in his book *Aspects of Christian Social Ethics* begins to show us a way out of our dilemma. "According to the Scriptural perspective, work becomes a waystation of spiritual witness and service, a daily traveled bridge between theology and social ethics. In other words, work for the believer is a sacred stewardship, and in fulfilling his job he will either accredit or violate the Christian witness."[6] Believers can and should think differently from everyone else in our culture about all aspects of life, especially work. Because we celebrate human creativity as evidence of our being made in the Creator's likeness, Christians must encourage one another to do work worthy of our best efforts and worthy of our high calling. As Dorothy Sayers put it, we must challenge one another to seek "the kingdom of a divine understanding of work"[7] which can, if we find it, give us a mysterious and glorious view of vocation and work.

The purpose of this book is to explore the Biblical intersection of faith and work, attempting to understand the differences between work, calling, and vocation and how they should be Biblically applied in our daily lives.

Os Guinness in his book *The Call* identifies *calling* as "the truth that God calls us to himself so decisively that everything we are, everything we do and everything we have is invested with a special devotion and dynamism lived out as a response to his summons and service."[8] Guinness differentiates between our *primary* and our *secondary* callings: "Our primary calling as followers of Christ is by Him, to Him, and for Him . . . . Our secondary calling, considering who God is as sovereign, is that everyone, everywhere, and in everything should think, speak, live, and act entirely for Him." Our primary calling should lead without fail to a number of secondary callings. We discern the difference between our primary calling "to be" and our secondary callings "to do" when we fully integrate God's call into all areas of life. For followers of Christ, these secondary callings should lead us to find our unique life purpose, in order to use our particular gifts and abilities to their utmost for God's glory.

While as Guinness suggests there are a number of secondary callings that flow out of our primary call to become a disciple of Christ, this book will focus on only one: our *vocational calling* (our work in the world). Unfortunately the Biblical understanding of vocational calling has been lost by the church in the 21st century.

When properly understood, this Biblical doctrine of work can give great insight and purpose to our daily work. In this book we will examine four areas related to the Biblical doctrine of work.

First, it will examine the Biblical understanding of work as outlined in the Old and New Testaments.

Second, it will look at the history of the doctrine of work as experienced by the church during the last 2000 years in an attempt to understand how the church has wandered so far from the Biblical truth about work.

Third, the book will define the Biblical principle of all work as *calling* and how we are to live our lives in the light of that truth.

Finally, this book will look to the future and offer some direction for rediscovering this lost Biblical doctrine of work and understanding how, if properly understood, our vocational calling can help Christians impact our communities, our cities, and our world by helping restore the culture to the glory of God.

CHAPTER 2

The Gospel,
The Kingdom and Our Calling:
What Does the Bible Say About Work?

Remember that Paradise wasn't a vacation—it was a vocation.[9]

—Stuart Briscoe

God is a worker. From the very beginning of the Scriptures we are faced with the inescapable fact that work is part of God's character and nature. Vocation is "integral not incidental to the mission of God."[10]

"The Bible begins with the announcement, In the beginning God created . . . not sat majestic in the heavens. He created. He did something. He made something. He fashioned heaven and earth. The week of creation was a week of work."[11] Work in different forms is mentioned over 800 times in the Bible, more than all the terms used for worship, music, praise, and singing combined.[12]

Scripture teaches five foundational ideas about work which we must understand in order to build a Christian view of work, vocation, and calling:

1. The Four-Chapter Gospel
2. The Cultural Mandate
3. The Kingdom of God
4. Common Grace
5. The Meaning of Success

The Four-Chapter Gospel:
Creation, Fall, Redemption, Restoration

Christians do not fully comprehend the Biblical concepts of work, calling, and vocation because we have lost the vision of the grand metanarrative told by the Bible. This metanarrative encompasses Creation, Fall, Redemption, and Restoration. It is sometimes called the Four-Chapter Gospel.

The comprehensive grand narrative of Scripture has been neglected because, "We have fragmented the Bible into bits—moral bits, systematic-theological bits, devotional bits, historical-critical bits, narrative bits, and homiletical bits."[13] We have so dissected and compartmentalized the Bible that we have lost sight of its great overarching story. As a result, bits and pieces of the Bible are absorbed into the prevailing cultural story, which then supplants the Bible as the story which shapes our lives. Only the unified Biblical narrative has the authority to enable us to withstand the competing humanist narrative currently shaping our culture.

Scripture begins with the creation of all things and ends with the renewal of all things, and in between it offers an interpretation of the meaning of all history. N.T. Wright says that the divine drama told in Scripture "offers a story which is the story of the whole world. It is public truth."[14] The Biblical metanarrative makes a comprehensive claim on all humanity, calling each one of us to find our place in His Story.

Despite the greatness of the Biblical narrative, in the past two centuries the church in the Western world has looked at the Bible from a different and more limited perspective. In the United States during the first half of the nineteenth century came the great religious revival called the Second Great Awakening. It was led by individual preachers such as Charles Finney, Lyman Beecher, Barton Stone, Peter Cartwright, and Asahel Nettleton.

The revivalist preachers' view of the gospel focused on personal sin and individual salvation. "Come forward and be saved," "Pray to receive Christ," "Walk with Jesus," and "Share your faith with other people" became the common language of Christian faith. While the movement had substantial positive effects, it led to a truncated gospel. Its view of Scripture can be called the Two-Chapter Gospel.

In the Two-Chapter Gospel, Chapter One presents our problem: separation from God because of our sin. Chapter Two presents the solution: Jesus Christ has come into the world to bring salvation and reunite us with God through His work on the cross.

While sin and salvation are undeniable realities, they are not the complete gospel. In this abridged version of the gospel, Christianity becomes all about *us*. The Two-Chapter Gospel ignores creation and the final restoration. It leaves out God's reason for our creation (which we will consider later as the Cultural Mandate) and the Christian's final destination.

We must understand the Bible teaches salvation is not an end in itself; it is a means to fulfill God's ultimate plan for man on this earth in this age. With creation edited out, the gospel becomes all about sinners being solicited for salvation. Tim Keller puts it this way:

Some conservative Christians think of the story of salvation as the fall, redemption, heaven. In this narrative, the purpose of redemption is escape from this world; only saved people have anything of value, while unbelieving people in the world are seen as blind and bad. If, however, the story of salvation is creation, fall, redemption, and restoration, then things look different. In this narrative, non-Christians are seen as created in the image of God and given much wisdom and greatness within them (cf. Ps. 8), even though the image is defaced and fallen. Moreover, the purpose of redemption is not to escape the world but to renew it . . . It is about the coming of God's kingdom to renew all things . . . if we lose the emphasis on conversion, we lose the power of the gospel for personal transformation. We will not work sacrificially and joyfully for justice. On the other hand, if we lose the emphasis on the corporate—on the kingdom—we lose the power of the gospel for cultural transformation.[15]

In his book *Creation Regained*, Albert Wolters encapsulates the gospel: "What was formed in creation has been historically deformed by sin and must be reformed in Christ."[16]

Mike Metzger sums up the shift from the Four-Chapter Gospel to the Two-Chapter Gospel in this way:

For two thousand years, the gospel was recited in four chapters titled creation, fall, redemption, and the final restoration. It reminds us that we are made in the image of God. This gospel started in Genesis One and can be found in the Apostles' and the Nicene Creed. Tragically, two hundred years ago the story was edited to two chapters; the fall and redemption. The opening chapter of creation was largely forgotten. The new starting line was Genesis Three. It reminds people that they are fallen sinners. We're both—made in God's image and sinners. Yet the two-chapter gospel accentuates our wounds. The four-chapter gospel elevates our worth as image-bearers of God. The two-chapter story focuses on our deficiency. The four-chapter story reminds us of our dignity.[17]

There is an important practical reason to read the Bible as one narrative: it enables us to understand our identity as God's people as we see our role in His story. From this perspective we clearly see our call to participate in God's redemptive mission.

Chris Wright summarizes this missional Biblical narrative: "The whole Bible renders to us the story of God's mission through God's people in their engagement with God's world for the sake of God's whole creation."[18] Thus the mission of the people of God is "our committed participation as God's people, at God's invitation and command, in God's own mission within the history of God's world for the redemption of God's creation."[19]

Our identity as God's people comes from our missional role in the Biblical story, which is not future, but in the here and now. By recovering Scripture's storyline we rediscover our true identity.

As we go through our lives in this world, we must realize we are on a mission from God. Our mission goes beyond evangelizing far-off places or teaching a Sunday School class. It defines the meaning of our entire lives, which necessarily means that it encompasses our vocational work.

Faithfulness to our identity as God's missional people allows us to *not* be conformed to the cultural idolatry of this world but to *be* transformed by the gospel of Christ (Romans 12:2). By answering the call to fulfill our roles in God's redemptive drama, we find meaning in even the most mundane activities. Along with meaning we find peace and satisfaction which transcend our greatest expectations.

Stressing the urgency of reading the Bible as one unified story, Michael Goheen said:

> The question is not whether the whole of our lives will be shaped by some grand story. The only question is which grand story will shape our lives. For the one who has heard Jesus' call to follow him, the call comes with a summons to enter the story of which he was the climactic moment—the story narrated in the Bible. It is an invitation to find our place in that story. The issue is urgent: only then can we submit to Scripture's authority; only then can we understand our missional identity; only then can we resist being absorbed into the dangerous idolatries of our time. The church needs pastors and leaders, (businesses needs entrepreneurs and workers) and the academy needs scholars and teachers who are in the grip of this story, and discharge their task in a way that calls church members and students to find their place in the true story of the world.[20]

The gospel, when understood in its fullness, is not solely about individual happiness and fulfillment; it is not all about me. "It is not just a wonderful plan for 'my life' but a wonderful plan for the world; it is about the coming of God's kingdom to renew all things."[21] Only with this bigger picture in view can we understand how *our story* fits into *His story.*

The Cultural Mandate

We were created to be stewards of God's creation through our work. The opening two chapters of Genesis provide a foundation for how God sees work, culture, and man's responsibility. This same perspective extends throughout all the Scriptures.

In the beginning, prior to their Fall, God assigned Adam and Eve important work. "The LORD God took the man and put him in the Garden of Eden to work it and take care of it" (Genesis 2:15). Humanity was created by God to cultivate and keep God's creation, which included developing it and protecting it.

Work is not a curse but a gift from God. By our work we employ useful skills to glorify God and love our neighbors. Work is not a result of the Fall, although the Fall because of its curse made it inevitable that sometimes work would be frustrating and feel meaningless (Genesis 3:17-19).

In the story of creation, God brought order out of chaos. A gardener does something similar when he creatively uses the materials at his disposal and rearranges them to produce additional resources for mankind. Thus Adam's work in the garden can be seen as a metaphor for all work. A gardener is not a park ranger; he does not leave things in their natural state. With this idea in view, Tim Keller offers the following definition of *work:* "Rearranging the raw materials of a particular domain to draw out its potential for the flourishing of everyone."[22] That is what Adam was called to do in the garden, and that is what we are still called to do in our work today.

In the opening chapter of Genesis we find what is called the Cultural Mandate, also known as the Creation Mandate. "God blessed them and said to them, 'Be fruitful and increase in number; fill the earth and subdue it. Rule over the fish of the sea and the birds of the air and over every living creature that moves on the ground'" (Genesis 1:28). Nancy Pearcey in her book *Total Truth* interprets the Cultural Mandate:

> The first phrase, "be fruitful and multiply," means to develop the social world: build families, churches, schools, cities, governments, laws. The second phrase, "subdue the earth," means to harness the natural world: plant crops, build bridges, design computers, and compose music. This passage is sometimes called the Cultural Mandate because it tells us that our original purpose was to create cultures, build civilizations—nothing less.[23]

The Cultural Mandate was meant for not only Adam and Eve, but for us as well. It still stands as God's directive for our stewardship of His creation. Traditionally Christian theologians have understood Genesis 1:28 as mankind's purpose and permission for engaging the world. Doug Kelly writes, "Only because mankind was created in the image of God was it appropriate to grant him the awesome responsibility of dominion over the entire created order."[24]

And so from the very beginning our purpose has been bound up with our identity. We are creatures made in the image of God (Genesis 1:26-27). As beings made in God's image, we are meant to "image" God, that is, to reflect Him. Being in the image of God refers not only to who we *are* but also to what we are created to *do*. We are called not just to work but to do certain tasks to achieve a definite goal.

Genesis 1:28 commands us to be fruitful, increase, fill, subdue, and rule. These five commands reveal our most basic human responsibilities. Richard Pratt explains:

> It was God's design that people build an earthly culture for his glory. This Cultural Mandate involves two basic responsibilities: multiplication and dominion. First God gave Adam and Eve a commission to multiply: Be fruitful . . . increase . . . fill. Their job was to produce enough images of God to cover the earth. Second, God ordered them to exercise dominion over the earth: Fill . . . subdue . . . rule. Adam and Eve were to exercise authority over creation, managing its vast resources on God's behalf. Needless to say, these two mandates cannot be entirely separated from each other . . . . Nonetheless, from the beginning these two sides of the Cultural Mandate were to be our main tasks in life.[25]

How do we summarize the Cultural Mandate in a practical, workable manner? D. James Kennedy offers the following definition:

> We are to take all the potentialities of this world, all of its spheres and institutions, and bring them all to the glory of God. We are to use this world to the

glory of God. We are to bring it and surrender it at the foot of the Cross. In every aspect of the world, we are to bring glory to God and this means in all of the institutions of the world.[26]

Richard Pratt's claim that "God ordained humanity to be the primary instrument by which his kingship will be realized on earth"[27] leads him to a down-to-earth description of how the Cultural Mandate works:

The Great King has summoned each of us into his throne room. Take this portion of my kingdom, he says, I am making you my steward over your office, your workbench, your kitchen stove. Put your heart into mastering this part of my world. Get it in order; unearth its treasures; do all you can with it. Then everyone will see what a glorious King I am. That's why we get up every morning and go to work. We don't labor simply to survive, insects do that. Our work is an honor, a privileged commission from our great King. God has given each of us a portion of his kingdom to explore and to develop to its fullness.[28]

Nancy Pearcey expands on our working definition by describing the relationship between the Cultural Mandate and work:

The lesson of the Cultural Mandate is that our sense of fulfillment depends on engaging in creative, constructive work. The ideal human existence is not eternal leisure or an endless vacation—or even a monastic retreat into prayer and meditation—but creative effort expended for the glory of God and the benefit of others. Our calling is not just to "go to heaven" but also to cultivate the earth, not just to "save souls" but also to serve God through our work. For God himself is engaged not only in the work of salvation but also in the work of preserving and developing His creation. When we obey the Cultural Mandate, we participate in the work of God himself.[29]

Even after the Fall, when mankind and all creation was plunged into sin, we know that the Cultural Mandate was not nullified. God restated it to Noah after the flood (Genesis 8:15-9:17). In fact, nowhere does Scripture say that the Cultural Mandate has ever been revoked.

A strong argument can be made that Jesus' Great Commission (Matthew 28:18-20) is a restatement of the Cultural Mandate for His church. Theologians debate how the Cultural Mandate and the Great Commission fit together, but it is clear that both call for a renewal of culture.[30] These two great mandates should both hold sway over the Christian's life.

Theologian John Frame writes that having completed his redemptive work, Jesus rose (and we with him, Romans 6) to receive "all authority in heaven and on earth" (Matthew 28:18). Frame suggests that as the Cultural Mandate sent Adam and Eve to take dominion over the whole earth in God's name, so Christ calls his disciples to "Go and make disciples of all nations, baptizing them in the name of the Father and of the Son and of the Holy Spirit, and teaching them to obey everything that I have commanded you. And surely I am with you always, to the very end of the age" (Matthew 28:19-20).

> The difference between the Cultural Mandate and the Great Commission is that the former precedes the fall and the work of Christ; the latter follows these. Otherwise they are very much the same. Of course, it is not possible for people to subdue the earth for God until their hearts are changed by the Holy Spirit. So "taking dominion," following the Resurrection, begins with evangelism and baptism. But baptism is not the end, and evangelism is not simply bringing people to an initial profession of faith. It is making disciples and teaching them to observe comprehensively all that Jesus has commanded, with the assurance of Jesus' continuing presence. Jesus' commands deal not only with repentance, faith, and worship. They also concern our treatment of the poor, our sexual ethics, marriage and divorce, anger, love of enemies, fasting, anxiety, hypocrisy, and many other subjects.[31]

When people through faith embrace Christ, they should also be led to embrace the Cultural Mandate. They can then bring their new faith and desire to obey Christ into their daily work.

Paul identified Jesus as the *second man* and the *last Adam*, in contrast to the *first man* and the *first Adam* (1 Corinthians 15:45-49). The first Adam failed to carry out God's mandate. Now Jesus, the last Adam, is fulfilling the original mandate which God gave to humanity.

God commanded Adam and Eve to be fruitful, to multiply, to fill the earth, and to subdue it for God's glory. Jesus, the second Adam, has taken up that task. Just as the first Adam had a bride to serve as his helper (Genesis 2:18-25), so the second Adam has chosen a bride to serve as His helper. Jesus' bride is the church (Ephesians 5:29-32). Together with His bride, Jesus is fulfilling the original mandate by filling earth with regenerated images of God, who in turn submit to God's rule and subdue the earth for His glory.[32]

To state it a little differently, the Cultural Mandate which God gave to the first Adam and his bride has now become the Great Commission, which God has given to Christ (Isaiah 42:1-12; 49:1-26) and through Christ to the church (Matthew 28:18-20; Luke 24:45-49; Acts 1:8; 13:47; Romans 15:18).

The Cultural Mandate which God gave Adam and Eve also calls Christians to partner with Him in His work. From the beginning, God is prepared to entrust the "Garden" to man and for us to become His co-workers. Our stewardship role is a call for man to work with and for God. The significance of our work is directly related to its connection with God's work.

When you answer God's call to use your gifts in work, whether by making clothes, practicing law, tilling the field, mending broken bodies, or nurturing children, you are participating in God's work. God does not only send ministers to give the world sermons; He sends doctors to give medicine, teachers to impart wisdom and so on.

The Cultural Mandate is of such foundational importance for the whole of the Scriptural history of revelation, and therefore for a Biblical worldview, that we would do well to look more closely at its wording.[33] We are more than merely *permitted* to engage every part of the created order. We are told that the created world is *ours,* given to us as a trust from God Himself. We are to engage it, announcing and exercising the presence and rule of Christ over every part of it. This includes the arts and the sciences, social justice and economics, churches and U2 concerts, *The Passion of the Christ* and *Les Miserables.*

> Who formed the world of nature (which provides the raw material for physical sciences)? Who formed the universe of human interactions (which is the raw material of politics, economics, sociology, and history)? Who is the source of all harmony, form, and narrative pattern (which is the raw material for art)? Who is the source of the human mind (which is the raw material for philosophy and psychology)? And who, moment by moment, maintains the connection between our minds and the world beyond our minds? God did, God does.[34]

In conclusion, the Cultural Mandate was meant to govern everything Adam and Eve would do after it was given. As the social critic Herbert Schlossberg says, "The 'salt' of people changed by the gospel must change the world."[35] The gospel of Christ bids us to be faithful to the call of the Cultural Mandate. "By filling and ruling over the world, we fulfill our true purpose in life. We reach the heights of dignity because we represent and extend the authority of the King of the universe."[36]

Understanding the importance of the Cultural Mandate in our lives today is the first step in rediscovering the Biblical doctrine of work.

The Kingdom of God

Once we understand that the answer to the question "What were we created to do?" is the Cultural Mandate, the next logical question is "Where and when do we carry it out?"

All Christians realize that Jesus came to earth to be the perfect sacrifice for our sins, but few recognize that he also came to establish the Kingdom of God. Understanding our place in God's Kingdom is critical to understanding our vocational calling. Paul Stevens in his book *Doing God's Business* comments, "The New Testament treats work in the context of a larger framework: the call of God to live totally for him and his kingdom."[37]

After John the Baptist was put in prison, Jesus began his ministry in Galilee by proclaiming the good news and saying, "The time is fulfilled, and the kingdom of God is at hand; repent and believe in the gospel" (Mark 1:15 NASB). In this opening statement of Jesus' earthly ministry we find four of the most important words in the New Testament: *kingdom, gospel, repent,* and *believe.* Although these are familiar terms, most Christians would struggle to explain how *gospel, repent,* and *believe* relate to the Kingdom of God.

The word *kingdom* occurs 162 times in the New Testament. Clearly the Kingdom of God is central to the story of the Gospels. In fact we could make a strong argument that the Kingdom of God is central to the message of all the Scriptures. Every time we read of God as the Great King, of the Lordship of Christ, of divine sovereignty, authority and dominion, of command and obedience, of worship and honor, we are reading the language of the Kingdom.[38]

The idea of the Kingdom is woven into the fabric of both the Old and New Testaments. It consistently points to our sovereign King, Jesus Christ. "All the Biblical promises find their fulfillment in Jesus Christ. Every element of the Old Testament's unfolding revelation of the kingdom leads to the Person of Jesus Christ come in the flesh."[39]

The Kingdom of God is one of the pivotal themes of the whole Bible, to the extent that we could say the entire Bible is about Jesus and the Kingdom.[40] But what *is* the Kingdom of God?

In the most general sense, the Kingdom of God is the rule of the eternal sovereign God over all His creation (Psalm 103:19; Daniel 4:3). Yet in the New Testament, Jesus uses a much narrower definition of the Kingdom of God. The Kingdom of God is the fulfillment of the long-awaited Messianic rule predicted in the Old Testament (Psalm 2), although it has come in an unexpected way.

The coming of the Kingdom is the central event of redemptive history, which explains its prominent place in the teaching of Christ. "The kingdom of God is the age to come breaking in to the present age."[41]

The coming of the Kingdom of God involves two great moments. The first is a fulfillment within history with Christ's birth, life, death and resurrection; the second is the consummation of the Kingdom at the end of history with the second coming of Christ. George Ladd writes that God's plan "was not to bring the evil Age to its end and inaugurate the Age to Come. It was rather to bring the powers of the future Age to men in the midst of the present evil Age."[42]

George Ladd describes the mysterious nature of the Kingdom:

> The "mystery of the kingdom" is the key to the understanding of the unique element in Jesus' teaching about the Kingdom. He announced that the Kingdom of God had come near; in fact, he affirmed that it had actually come upon men (Mt. 12:28). It was present in his word and in his messianic works.

It was present in his person; it was present as the messianic salvation. It constituted a fulfillment of the OT expectation. Yet the coming and presence of the Kingdom was not self-explanatory and altogether self-evident. There was something about it which could be understood only by revelation. This meant that while the presence of the Kingdom was a fulfillment of the OT expectation, it was a fulfillment in different terms from those which one might expect from the prophets. Before the end of the age and the coming of the Kingdom in glorious power, it was God's purpose that the powers of that eschatological Kingdom should enter into human history to accomplish a defeat of Satan's kingdom, and to set at work the dynamic power of God's redemptive reign among men [cf. II Cor. 5:17]. This new manifestation of God's Kingdom was taking place on the level of human history and centered in one man—Jesus Christ.[43]

The answer to the question "What is the Kingdom?" raises another question: *"When* is the Kingdom?"

Many passages in the New Testament lead us to believe that the Kingdom is *here already.* A large part of Christ's ministry was the announcement of the coming of the Kingdom of God (Matthew 4:17, 23; 10:7; 24:14; Luke 4:43). At the same time, other New Testament references lead us to believe that the Kingdom is *not yet.* The apostle John in his vision heard of a time when "The kingdom of the world has become the kingdom of our Lord and of his Christ, and he will reign for ever and ever" (Revelation 11:15) and a time when the hosts of darkness face crushing defeat (Revelation 19:11-21). Paul announced a time when every knee will bow to Jesus and every tongue confess Him as Lord (Philippians 2:10-11). Other passages speak of believers inheriting the Kingdom at the end, which would indicate that the Kingdom of God will arrive at the end of this present age (Matthew 25:34; Colossians 1:12; James 2:5).

We can reconcile the apparent contradiction by acknowledging that Christians today live in the tension of the *already, not yet*. The Kingdom of God has *already* been established here on earth through the life, death, and resurrection of Jesus Christ; but it has *not yet* been consummated. The consummation will happen at the end of this present age when Jesus Christ physically returns to bring both peace and judgment and to usher in the New Heaven and New Earth.

One twentieth-century theologian compared the coming of the Kingdom to World War II between the Allies and Germany.[44] For all intents and purposes, World War II in Europe was over on D-Day, when Allied troops established a beachhead in Normandy, France. Everyone, even the Germans, knew that V-E Day was inevitable, when the war would end with Germany's defeat. All that remained was for the Allies to liberate Europe. Yet between D-Day and V-E Day came the Battle of the Bulge, a desperate counterattack by the German army, fought during one of the worst winters in European history. For six weeks the battle raged back and forth. It was the deadliest battle for American forces during the war; over 19,000 Americans were killed.

In terms of the Kingdom of God, Christ's first coming was D-Day. It was the decisive invasion of the war, guaranteeing the enemy's eventual defeat. The second coming of Christ will be V-E Day, in which the enemy finally lays down its arms and surrenders.[45]

When Christ died on the cross for our sins and was resurrected on the third day, He struck a death blow to sin, death, and Satan and established the Kingdom of God. That Kingdom will be consummated when Christ returns at His second coming. Yet Christians today live our lives between D-Day and V-E Day, in the Battle of the Bulge. The outcome of the conflict is certain and our victory is sure, but the enemy is throwing everything at the army of God in the fiercest battle of the war.

We must see our vocational calling within the context of this final great battle. Cornelius Plantinga in his book *Engaging God's World* talks about the struggle of fulfilling our work in the Kingdom:

> A Christian who goes to work for the kingdom (that's every Christian) simultaneously goes to war. What's needed on God's side are well-educated warriors (warriors who know what's going on). We are now fallen creatures in a fallen world. The Christian gospel tells us that all hell has broken loose in this sad world and that, in Christ, all heaven has come to do battle. Christ has come to defeat the powers and principalities, to move the world over onto a new foundation, and to equip a people— informed, devout, determined people—to lead the way in righting what's wrong, transforming what's corrupted, in doing things that make for peace, expecting these things will travel across the border from this world to the new heaven and earth.[46]

"The kingdom of God, therefore, is to be understood as the reign of God dynamically active in human history through Jesus

Christ, the purpose of which is the redemption of his people from sin and from demonic powers, and the final establishment of the new heavens and the new earth."[47]

God's people should be encouraged, knowing that God has brought the powers of the age to come into our midst. He has done this through the ministry, death, and resurrection of Christ and the saving and empowering presence of His Spirit. Yet we must be careful not to overemphasize the present reign of God at the cost of the future and final coming of His reign at the end of this age.

We must also understand that our duty as members of the Kingdom is not to bring the Kingdom into existence, nor is the Kingdom something we build ourselves. The Kingdom is brought and built by the King.

When it speaks of the Kingdom, the New Testament uses verbs like *receive, inherit, enter,* and *work.* We are called to enter into it by faith in Christ alone and to pray that we may be enabled more and more to submit ourselves to the beneficent rule of God in every area of our lives. The Kingdom is not man's upward climb to perfection; it is God's breaking into human history to establish his reign and to advance his purposes.[48] In the Lord's Prayer, when we pray *Thy Kingdom come,* "We pray that Satan's kingdom may be destroyed; and that the kingdom of grace may be advanced, ourselves and others brought into it, and kept in it; and the kingdom of glory may be hastened."[49]

We understand that it is God, through His providence, who is establishing His Kingdom here on earth. Yet this does not imply that we lack responsibility for the part that God has called us to play. Much of what God accomplishes, He does through secondary means, and frequently His people are those secondary means. The bottom line is that "when the world appears to be aimlessly tumbled about, the Lord is everywhere at work"[50] often using the work of His people to bring about His Kingdom.

Despite all the New Testament references to the Kingdom, most evangelical Christians today have no idea that their daily work has anything to do with the Kingdom of God. Paul Marshall in his book *Heaven Is Not My Home* argues that the escapist attitude of many American Christians has been shaped by a false eschatology which teaches that our eternal destiny is in heaven. In this viewpoint, our salvation is like a one-way bus ticket to heaven, and the earth is only a bus stop. It does not really matter what we do while we wait for the bus.

The Scriptures teach a different reality. *Heaven* is actually the bus stop! There God's people await the return of the King who will consummate the Kingdom which He inaugurated at His first coming. Then He will fulfill the Biblical promise of a new heavens and a new earth. "Our destiny is an earthly one: a new earth, an earth redeemed and transfigured. An earth reunited with heaven, but an earth, nevertheless."[51]

If the Kingdom of God is here and now in this present age, then what is our purpose in that Kingdom? Jesus told his followers, "You are the salt of the earth" and "You are the light of the world" (Matthew 5:13, 14). God has delivered each of His children out of death into life and out of darkness into light—for a reason. As we believe, repent, and enter into the Kingdom in this age, our lives become a witness to the way things *could* be and a signpost pointing to the way things *will* be in the new heaven and new earth.

Confessing with our mouths that "Jesus is Lord" should do more than shape our church life and a few spiritual habits here and there. As Kingdom people, we must be actively spreading God's reign into every segment of society. We should be influencing the world by bringing God's love and grace to all, whether through the arts, through business, through politics or through our other vocations.[52]

Nowhere in the New Testament is the Cultural Mandate's relationship to the Kingdom of God more apparent than in the second chapter of Hebrews. The author of the letter to Hebrews quotes Psalm 8, which paints a magnificent picture of what man was created to be (Hebrews 2:6-8). Here mankind fully embraced the Cultural Mandate to have dominion over all things. That is the way it was at the creation; that is the way it was supposed to be. Then the writer of Hebrews says, "Yet at present we do not see everything subject to them [humanity]." The author points to the startling contrast between the way things were and the way things are because of the Fall. Paul wrote that "sin entered the world through one man, and death through sin, and in this way death came to all people, because all sinned" (Romans 5:12). The reign of sin and death caused by the Fall prevented man from fully carrying out the work God created him for in the garden.

Fallen man cannot fulfill the Cultural Mandate. Sin did not abrogate the Cultural Mandate, but it made man unable to fulfill it. The author of Hebrews offers hope in one of the most striking lines in the letter: "But we do see Jesus, who was made lower than the angels for a little while, now crowned with glory and honor because he suffered death, so that by the grace of God he might taste death for everyone" (Hebrews 2:9).

As the second Adam, Jesus lived the perfect life on earth that the first Adam could not live. Through that perfect life Jesus became the Psalm 8 man, perfectly fulfilling the Cultural Mandate. It is through His life, death, and resurrection that all of those who are in Him stand restored in the place of the first Adam with the ability to once again fulfill the Cultural Mandate.

John Frame summarizes it this way:

> Redemption should be interpreted as God's reparation of Adam's failure and fulfillment of his original creation mandate through the Second Adam, Jesus the Messiah. Whereas the first Adam betrayed his heavenly Father and fell into sin by snatching after divinity (Gen. 3:4-6), the Second Adam proved his perfect loyalty by assuming the posture of a servant and humbling himself even unto the death of the cross (Matt. 4:1-11; Phil. 2:5-11). And by his perfect life and spotless sacrifice Jesus became a vicarious atonement for sin and undid the evil that the first Adam initiated. Moreover, the Second Adam is currently fulfilling the original mandate God had given to humanity.[53]

The salvation Christ has offered through His life, death, and resurrection makes it possible for Christians to enter into the Kingdom in this present age and fulfill the Cultural Mandate to the great glory of our King, furthering His Kingdom here on earth. Until we understand our place in God's Kingdom, we will never fully understand the importance of the work that He has called us to do in our present lives.

Common Grace

The Cultural Mandate dictates that mankind has a responsibility to be stewards of the creation, both in the sphere of nature and the sphere of culture. After the Fall and the curse of sin, this endeavor became much more difficult (Genesis 3:17-19). Yet because God restated the Cultural Mandate to Noah after the flood (Genesis 9:1), we know that it has not been abrogated. Our job is still to do whatever we can to shape creation to reflect God's glory. Christians are still called to fill and subdue the earth, to transform the world and put everything under the Lordship of Christ until he comes again.

As Christians fulfill this mission vocationally, we will find ourselves working together with non-Christians for common political, economic, or cultural causes. We should understand the Biblical basis for commonality between believer and unbeliever.

Biblically there is precedent for believers cooperating with non-believers to achieve ends under the Cultural Mandate. Joseph worked with the Egyptians to alleviate famine (Genesis 41). Daniel served faithfully in Nebuchadnezzar's court (Daniel 2).

Jeremiah wrote to the Jewish exiles in Babylon to "seek the peace and prosperity of the city to which I have carried you into exile. Pray to the Lord for it, because if it prospers, you too will prosper" (Jeremiah 29:7). Paul told the Galatians, "as we have opportunity, let us do good to all people, especially to those who belong to the family of believers" (Galatians 6:10).

At the same time, there is other Scripture which seems to say the opposite. When the Israelites escaped from Egypt, "they plundered the Egyptians" (Exodus 12:35-36). Paul admonished the Corinthians, "Do not be yoked together with unbelievers. For what do righteousness and unrighteousness have in common? Or what fellowship can light have with darkness?" (2 Corinthians 6:14). When the Jews returned from Babylon, the Samaritans were not allowed to help the people of God rebuild the temple (Ezra 4:1-3). Being "in the world but not of the world" is more complicated than it first appears![54]

James wrote, "Every good and perfect gift is from above, coming down from the Father of the heavenly lights, who does not change like shifting shadows" (James 1:17). Referring to this passage, Tim Keller writes in his book *The Reason for God:*

> This means that no matter who performs it, every
> act of goodness, wisdom, justice, and beauty is
> empowered by God. God gives out good gifts of
> wisdom, talent, beauty, and skill "graciously"—
> that is, in a completely unmerited way. He casts
> them across all humanity, regardless of religious
> conviction, race, gender, or any other attribute to
> enrich, brighten, and preserve the world.[55]

The Scriptures talk about God's grace in two fundamentally different ways. The first is what theologians call *special grace*. It is the favor of God which actually results in salvation.

Special grace is the work of the Holy Spirit in calling, regenerating, justifying, and sanctifying individual sinners. Special grace is restricted to those who actually come to saving faith in Jesus Christ through the work of the Holy Spirit. The Dutch theologian Herman Bavinck described the special grace of God as "his voluntary, unrestrained, unmerited favor toward guilty sinners, granting them justification and life instead of the penalty of death, which they deserved."[56] J. I. Packer expressed it this way:

> The grace of God is love freely shown towards
> guilty sinners, contrary to their merit and indeed
> in defiance of their demerit. It is God showing
> goodness to persons who deserve only severity, and
> had no reason to expect anything but severity.[57]

Yet as Keller implies, special grace is not the only manifestation of God's grace to this fallen world. Could those who never come to saving faith in Jesus Christ be recipients of another type of divine grace?

The apostle Paul described the universal condition of humanity in bleak terms. In the book of Romans he wrote, "There is no one righteous, not even one; there is no one who understands, no one who seeks God. All have turned away, they have together become worthless; there is no one who does good, not even one" (Romans 3:10-12). Theologians call this fallen state, apart from Christ, *total depravity.*

But total depravity is not utter depravity. We are not as wicked as we possibly could be. We observe unbelievers enjoying God's gifts and doing things which benefit the world. As John Murray observed, the idea of total depravity forces us to deal with thorny questions:

> How is it that men who still lie under the wrath and curse of God and are heirs of hell enjoy so many good gifts at the hand of God? How is it that men who are not savingly renewed by the Spirit of God nevertheless exhibit so many qualities, gifts and accomplishments that promote the preservation, temporal happiness, cultural progress, social and economic improvement of themselves and of others? How is it that races and peoples that have been apparently untouched by the redemptive and regenerative influences of the gospel contribute so much to what we call human civilization? To put the question most comprehensively: how is it that this sin-cursed world enjoys so much favour and

kindness at the hand of its holy and ever-blessed Creator?[58]

The great reformer John Calvin was one of the first to suggest that the answers to these questions are found in the distinction the Bible draws between God's *special* or *saving grace* and His *common* or *non-saving grace.* Calvin described the capacity for goodness in the non-Christian as a gift from God. He said that an unbelieving mind, "though fallen and perverted from its wholeness, is nevertheless clothed and ornamented with God's excellent gifts."[59] The concept of common grace is also seen in a number of the Reformed Confessions written and further developed by later theologians such as Abraham Kuyper, Herman Bavinck, and John Murray.

Common grace was defined by Abraham Kuyper as "that act of God by which He negatively curbs the operations of Satan, death, and sin, and by which He positively creates an intermediate state for this cosmos, as well as for our human race, which is and continues to be deeply and radically sinful, but in which sin cannot work out its end."[60] John Murray defined common grace as "every favour of whatever kind or degree, falling short of salvation, which this undeserving and sin-cursed world enjoys at the hand of God."[61]

Common grace is *common* because it is universal; it is *grace* because it is undeserved and given by a gracious God. So although one cannot do good in the fullest sense without the blessings of God's special grace, one can carry out the commandments of God in an external and temporary fashion. We see examples of unbelieving people doing this in many places in the Scriptures. By common grace a person can choose to commit sins which are relatively less wicked than others. Murray offered this example: "The ploughing of the wicked is sin, but it is more sinful for the wicked not to plough."[62]

The Westminster Confession of Faith firmly distinguishes between *saving grace* and *common grace:*

> Although the works done by unregenerate men may in themselves be things which God commands and things which are useful to themselves and others, yet—because they do not come from a heart purified by faith, are not done in a right manner according to the Word, and are not done for the right purpose, which is to glorify God—they are therefore sinful, and cannot please God or make one suitable to receive his grace. Yet, neglecting them is even more sinful and displeasing to God.[63]

In what follows we will examine three ways in which common grace manifests itself in the world.

First, through common grace *God restrains sin.* Jonathan Edwards said, "If sin was not restrained, it would immediately turn the soul into a fiery oven, or a furnace of fire and brimstone."[64] God's common grace prevents fallen human beings from doing all the wrong they could do. For example, God prevented others from killing Cain (Genesis 4:15). He prevented Abimelech king of Gerar from sexual sin with Abraham's wife Sarah (Genesis 20:6). He prevented Sennacherib king of Assyria from doing all the harm to Israel that he had planned (2 Kings 19:27-28). He protected His own Son Jesus from harm until the time for His death arrived. He now restrains "the secret power of lawlessness" (2 Thessalonians 2:7). He holds even Satan in check, allowing him to go only so far and no farther (Job 1:12; 2:6). Common grace keeps our total depravity from becoming absolute; it keeps the world from falling into anarchy.

Second, through common grace *God restrains His wrath against sinful mankind.* John Frame notes that it is surprising that human beings receive any blessing from God at all:

> God would have acted justly if he had destroyed the human race after the Fall. But instead he allowed human life to continue, promising redemption by the offspring of the woman (Gen. 3:15). And throughout Scripture we see that God does not give people the awesome punishment they deserve. Murray points out that God restrains the painful effects of the curse: of the thorns and thistles (Gen. 3:17) and of the wild beasts (Gen. 9:2, 5). God sometimes "overlooks" disobedience (Acts 17:30; cf. 14:16; Rom. 3:25). In the Old Testament period, he permitted divorce because of Israel's hardness of heart (Matt. 19:8), even though he hates divorce (Mal. 2:16).[65]

At the end of this age Christ will return, all wrongs will be righted, and God will punish all sin, either by punishing the offender or by placing the offender's sins on Jesus. The fact that this final judgment is still to come is another example of God's restraint through His common grace. He postpones His judgment in order to give people an opportunity to repent: "He is patient with you, not wanting anyone to perish, but everyone to come to repentance" (2 Peter 3:9). Common grace even restrains evil by placing restraints on the consequences of sin. For example, even though the ground is cursed due to the sin of Adam, it still brings forth enough to sustain mankind.

Third, through common grace *God bestows His blessings, both physical and spiritual, on all of mankind, including those who will reject Christ.* "He causes his sun to rise on the evil and the good, and sends rain on the righteous and the unrighteous" (Matthew 5:45). God blessed the Egyptian overseer's house for Joseph's sake (Genesis 39:5). Paul preached to pagan worshipers, "In the past, he let all nations go their own way. Yet he has not left himself without testimony: He has shown kindness by giving you rain from heaven and crops in their seasons; he provides you with plenty of food and fills your hearts with joy" (Acts 14:16-17). David marveled at God's bounty in creation:

> You care for the land and water it; you enrich it abundantly.
> The streams of God are filled with water to provide the people with grain, for so you have ordained it.
> You drench its furrows and level its ridges; you soften it with showers and bless its crops.
> You crown the year with your bounty, and your carts overflow with abundance.
> The grasslands of the desert overflow; the hills are clothed with gladness.
> The meadows are covered with flocks and the valleys are mantled with grain; they shout for joy and sing.
> (Psalm 65:9-13)

John Murray went on to say that God not only restrains evil in unredeemed men, He also endows them with:

... gifts, talents, and aptitudes; he stimulates them with interest and purpose to the practice of virtues, the pursuance of worthy tasks, and the cultivation of arts and sciences that occupy the time, activity and energy of men and that make for the benefit and civilization of the human race. He ordains institutions for the protection and promotion of right, the preservation of liberty, the advance of knowledge and the improvement of physical and moral conditions. We may regard these interests, pursuits and institutions as exercising both an expulsive and impulsive influence. Occupying the energy, activity and time of men they prevent the indulgence of less noble and ignoble pursuits and they exercise an ameliorating, moralizing, stabilizing and civilizing influence upon the social organism.[66]

Common grace empowers the non-Christian firefighter to go up the stairs of the Twin Towers on 9/11 to save a financial worker. Common grace motivates the non-Christian soldier to throw himself on a grenade and sacrifice his own life to save his comrades. However, Murray reminds us that "the good attributed to unregenerate men is after all only relative good. It is not good in the sense of meeting in motivation, principle and aim the requirements of God's law and the demands of his holiness."[67]

John Frame writes:

To please God, our works must be done to the glory of God, obedient to the Word of God, motivated by faith and love of God. Unbelievers never do good works in this sense; indeed, even believers' works always fall short according to this standard. But unbelievers are able to do things that look good to us. They don't look good to God, for God knows the heart. But they look good to us, and they often bring benefits to society. So non-Christians often improve society through their skills and ideas. They make scientific discoveries, produce labor-saving inventions, develop businesses that supply jobs, produce works of art and entertainment.[68]

We have looked at three ways in which common grace manifests itself in the world. Next we can ask, what is the *purpose* of common grace? Wayne Grudem in his book *Bible Doctrine: Essential Teachings of the Christian Faith* suggests four reasons for common grace.[69]

The first purpose of common grace is *to redeem those who will be saved.* Common grace serves the purpose of special or saving grace, and saving grace has as its specific end the glorification of the whole body of God's elect, which in turn has its ultimate end in the glory of God's name.[70] Without common grace, redemptive grace would be impossible because there would be nothing left of the human race from which to make children of God.[71] Either we would have been destroyed by God, or else we would have destroyed ourselves.

The second purpose of common grace is *to demonstrate God's mercy and goodness,* which are seen not only in the gift of salvation to believers but also in the blessing He gives to all people. David said, "The Lord is good to all; his compassion is over all that he has made"

(Psalm 145:9). When Jesus met the rich young ruler, He "looked at him and loved him" (Mark 10:21) even though the man rejected what Jesus told him and walked away. The fact that God delays judgment is another example of his mercy. God said through Ezekiel, "I take no pleasure in the death of the wicked, but rather that they turn from their ways and live" (Ezekiel 33:11). The apostle Paul tells us that God "wants all men to be saved and to come to a knowledge of the truth" (1 Timothy 2:4). By delaying punishment, God shows that He finds no pleasure in executing His final judgment, but rather delights in the salvation of men and women.

The third purpose of common grace is *to demonstrate God's justice*. Paul wrote in his letter to Romans that "The wrath of God is being revealed from heaven against all the godlessness and wickedness of men who suppress the truth by their wickedness, since what may be known about God is plain to them, because God has made it plain to them" (Romans 1:18-19). Through God's common grace, all people know the truth about God, yet they have "exchanged the truth of God for a lie" (Romans 1:25), leaving them without excuse. Paul went on to warn sinful people, "because of your stubbornness and your unrepentant heart, you are storing up wrath against yourself for the day of God's wrath, when his righteous judgment will be revealed" (Romans 2:5). In the light of such stubborn rejection of God's revealed truth, we see the justice of His condemnation even more clearly.

Finally, the fourth purpose of common grace is *to demonstrate God's glory* in the many ways His common grace actively operates in the lives of all human beings. As mankind exercises dominion over the earth, through common grace they "demonstrate and reflect the wisdom of their Creator, demonstrate Godlike qualities of skill and moral virtue and authority over the universe and so forth."[72]

Even though their motives are sinful, unbelievers still reflect the excellence of their Creator and bring glory to God in an imperfect but significant way.

God also uses common grace to work out His redemptive plan for His creation. Paul was a student who sat at the feet of the Jewish teacher Gamaliel (Acts 22:3). Moses grew up in Pharaoh's court and learned the wisdom of the Egyptians (Acts 7:22). "Long lines of preparation in the realm of 'Common Grace,' designed in the plan of God's all-comprehending providence, have fitted the most blessed of God's servants for the particular role they were to play in the kingdom of God."[73] Again John Murray states, "Of one thing we are sure that the glory of God is displayed in all his works and the glory of his wisdom, goodness, longsuffering, kindness and mercy is made known in the operations of his common grace."[74]

An appreciation for common grace enables us to effectively pursue relationships, evangelism, work, cultural engagement, and arts and entertainment through positive interaction with all of God's creation. Common grace gives us both a theological and a practical answer to how we can work to fulfill the Cultural Mandate with those who are not followers of Jesus Christ, while not becoming "of the world." Chuck Colson writes:

> God cares not only about redeeming souls but also about restoring his creation. He calls us to be agents not only of his saving grace but also of his common grace. Our job is not only to build up the church but also to build a society to the glory of God. As agents of God's common grace, we are called to help sustain and renew his creation, to uphold the created institutions of family and society, to pursue science

and scholarship, to create works of art and beauty, and to heal and help those suffering from the results of the Fall.[75]

Historically the Biblical understanding of both the Cultural Mandate and common grace has been a significant factor in the growth and spread of Christianity throughout the world. As believers who are created in the image of God, committed to God's glory, and called to be a light on a hill, we bear the responsibility to redeem not only personal souls, but entire cultures.[76]

Common grace is one of the means by which Christians serve the common good of their neighbors and transform the culture. It allows us to work alongside non-Christians for a common purpose. In this regard Abraham Kuyper writes:

> God is glorified in the total development toward which human life and power over nature gradually march on under the guardianship of "common grace." It is His created order, His work, that unfold here. It was He who seeded the field of humanity with all these powers. Without a "Common Grace" the seed which lay hidden in that field would never have come up and blossomed. Thanks to "Common Grace," it germinated, burgeoned, shot up high and will one day be in full flower, to reward not man but the heavenly Farmer . . . . A finished world will glorify God as builder and supreme Craftsman. What paradise was in bud will appear in full bloom.[77]

John Calvin insisted that it is the Spirit of God who establishes all human competence in arts and sciences "for the common good of mankind" and that common grace is a tool given by God that should not be neglected. "But if the Lord has willed that we be helped in physics, dialectic, mathematics, and other like disciplines, by the work and ministry of the ungodly, let us use this assistance. For if we neglect God's gift freely offered in these arts, we ought to suffer punishment for our sloths."[78]

We often meet people who are not Christians but who agree with a Christian stance on a certain cultural issue, and therefore they are willing to work together with Christians toward resolution. We should be open to working with them for a common goal. Francis Schaeffer popularized the use of the term *co-belligerence* to express the idea that the enemy of my enemy is my friend. He explained, "A co-belligerent is a person with whom I do not agree on all sorts of vital issues, but who, for whatever reasons of their own, is on the same side in a fight for some specific issue of public justice."[79]

Schaeffer emphasized the importance of avoiding the extremes of separatism on one side and compromise with non-believers on the other side.

> Christians must realize that there is a difference between being a co-belligerent and being an ally. At times we will seem to be saying exactly the same things as those without a Christian base are saying . . . . We must say what the Bible says when it causes us to seem to be saying what others are saying . . . . But we must never forget that this is only a passing co-belligerency and not an alliance.[80]

Although "we must be careful though that we do not become a stumbling block for other Christians, and that our co-belligerence does not communicate to a watching world the possibility of neutrality and the dilution of the exclusivity of Christ and the gospel,"[81] we must not miss opportunities presented to us through God's providence to further the Kingdom. According to Al Mohler, president of Southern Baptist Theological Seminary:

> We must be ready to stand together in cultural co-belligerence, rooted in a common core of philosophical and theological principles, without demanding confessional agreement or pretending that this has been achieved. We must contend for the right of Christian moral witness in secular society. We indeed need to be as wise as serpents and as innocent as doves to know how to contend for Christian truth.[82]

The Christian employee, surrounded by non-Christians at work, can take great hope from the doctrine of common grace. "Common grace helps us to acknowledge that there are times to embrace culture warmly, and times to be in stark, prophetic opposition to it. And the only durable, Biblical way to do both is to see culture through the lens of common grace."[83] This doctrine helps us make a strong Biblical case for engaging the culture while embracing the gospel.

Speaking of His Father in heaven, Jesus said, "He causes his sun to rise on the evil and the good, and sends rain on the righteous and the unrighteous" (Matthew 5:45). With this in mind, John Frame encourages us to see God's blessings everywhere:

> Every bit of food, every bit of rain and sunshine,
> comes from the goodness of our heavenly Father.
> God really does love us; he seeks our good. And
> while the Last Judgment tarries, God seeks the good
> of the reprobate as well. Thus, we should praise his
> name.[84]

Wherever we work, we can rest assured that God can use us through our vocational calling to influence our fellow employees, our company, our city, our nation, and the world for the glory of God.

The Biblical Meaning of Success

Two great lies have been promoted in our culture over the last twenty years. They are told to children in school, students in college and throughout the business world. The first great lie is "If you work hard enough, you can be anything you want to be." It is often sold as the American Dream, expressed in sayings such as "In America, anyone can grow up to be President." The second great lie is like the first one, yet possibly even more damaging: "You can be the best in the world." These lies are accepted by many Christians as well as non-Christians. They have done catastrophic damage to our view of work and vocation because they have distorted our Biblical view of success.

The pervasiveness of the two lies is revealed in *The Dip: A Little Book That Teaches You When to Quit and When to Stick,* the 2007 best-seller by popular business author Seth Godin. Godin establishes one of the book's foundational presuppositions in the following story:

Hanna Smith is a very lucky woman. She's a law clerk at the Supreme Court. She's the best in the world. Last year more that forty-two thousand people graduated from law school in the United States. And thirty-seven of them were awarded Supreme Court clerkships . . . . any one of the forty-two thousand who graduated from law school last year could have had Hanna's job.[85]

Now Hanna Smith is a very lucky woman, but she is also very talented and has worked diligently to have the opportunity to clerk for a Supreme Court Justice. Of the 42,000 people who graduated from law school that year, only a small percentage have the God—given talent, skills, and drive to qualify for this premiere position. Godin's underlying presupposition supports the two great lies, "If you work hard enough, you can be anything you want to be" and "You can be the best in the world." These lies are defining success in 21st century Western culture.

Success, defined as *being the master of your own destiny,* has become an idol of our culture. New York City pastor, Tim Keller, describes the idol in these words:

More than other idols, personal success and achievement lead to a sense that we ourselves are God, that our security and value rest in our own wisdom, strength and performance. To be the very best at what you do, to be at the top of the heap, means no one is like you. You are supreme.[86]

If we are to rediscover the Biblical doctrine of work, and if we are to correctly understand our own personal vocational calling, we must recognize how the Bible defines *success*.

The late John Wooden, the most successful college basketball coach in the history of the game and a committed Christian, was once asked how he would define success. He replied, "Success is peace of mind which is a direct result of self-satisfaction in knowing you did your best to become the best that you are capable of becoming."[87]

The New Testament defines success in a similar way in a story which Jesus told, known as the Parable of the Talents (Matthew 25:14-30). This parable offers profound Biblical insight not only into the definition of success, but into purpose of our call to work.

To fully understand the Parable of the Talents, we must see it in its larger context. Jesus taught this parable to His disciples during the last week of His ministry, only days before the crucifixion. On Tuesday of Holy Week, Jesus entered the temple for the last time and delivered a powerful sermon condemning the Pharisees. As Jesus and the disciples were leaving, one of the disciples commented on the majesty and glory of Herod's temple. Jesus' response must have surprised and shocked the disciples. "'Do you see all these things?' he asked. 'I tell you the truth, not one stone here will be left on another; every one will be thrown down'" (Matthew 24:2).

Troubled by this exchange, a short time later the disciples came to Jesus privately while they were resting on the Mount of Olives and asked Him two questions. "'Tell us,' they said, 'when will this happen, and what will be the sign of your coming and of the end of the age?'" (Matthew 24:3).

Jesus' response is known as the Olivet Discourse, found in Matthew 24, Mark 13, and Luke 21. Jesus' teaching refers primarily to the future periods of tribulation (including the destruction of the temple and the city of Jerusalem in 70 A.D.) and the second coming of Christ at the end of this current age. This extended discourse also includes practical instructions on how the disciples were to conduct their lives after the Master had departed. In Matthew's account, Jesus illustrates His teaching on these matters with a series of parables showing that there will be a delay before His return and explaining how Christians should live and work during the period between His first and second comings. The Olivet Discourse is the context for the Parable of the Talents.

The Parable of the Talents teaches that the kingdom of heaven will be like a man going on a long journey. Before he leaves, he gives his three servants different amounts of money. To the first he gives five talents, to the second he gives two talents, and to the last he gives only one talent.

Whatever its exact value, in the New Testament a *talent* indicates a large sum of money,[88] maybe even as much as a million dollars in today's currency.[89]

When the master returned from his travels, he asked his servants to give an account of the money he had given them. The first servant, who had been given five talents, reported that he had earned five additional talents. The master praised the servant, saying, "Well done, good and faithful servant. You have been faithful over a little; I will set you over much. Enter into the joy of your master" (Matthew 25:21 ESV).

The second servant, who had received two talents, gave a different account. He reported to the master that he had earned two more talents. The master praised this servant exactly the same way as the first, calling him good and faithful, giving him more responsibility, and inviting the servant into the joy of the master.

The last servant, who had received only one talent, reported that because he knew his master was a hard man, he buried his talent in the ground so he would be assured of returning the original amount to his master. The master called this servant wicked and lazy, saying that he should have at least placed the money in the bank where it would have generated some interest. The master commanded that the one talent be taken away from the last servant and given to the servant with ten talents. "For everyone who has will be given more, and he will have an abundance. Whoever does not have, even what he has will be taken from him" (Matthew 25:29). The master then ordered the lazy, wicked servant to be severely punished.

The Parable of the Talents describes what our work should look like while we wait for the return of Christ and the final consummation of His Kingdom. The preceding parable, the Parable of the Ten Virgins (Matthew 25:1-13), stressed the importance of being ready for the return of Christ. The Parable of the Talents gives us a picture of what this readiness looks like. "It is not to be passive waiting, but getting on with the job and making the most of the opportunities entrusted to us."[90]

As Christians we have a mission which our Lord expects us to accomplish in the here and now of this present age. As we have already seen, our mission is summarized in the Cultural Mandate. The stewardship of all we have been given is what we are called to do while we wait for our Savior's return. It is the dominion we are to exercise over all of God's creation; this is what we were made to do.

Prior to the Reformation, the medieval church interpreted the *talents* in Jesus' parable as spiritual gifts and graces which God bestows on Christians. Calvin helped shape the modern meaning of the word *talent* [91] by his revolutionary change in the interpretation of the Parable of the Talents, when he defined the talents as gifts from God in the form of a person's calling and natural ability.[92] Our talents are to be used for the common good and for God's glory. According to Calvin, God put us here to work in the Kingdom, and "the nature of the kingdom of Christ is that it every day grows and improves."[93]

Calvin made it clear that the use of our talents is not restricted to the church or to pious duties. It encompasses the whole of creation. Therefore Calvin's doctrine of *callings* emphasizes the utility, activity, and purposeful nature of God's work in the world. Alister McGrath suggests that for Calvin:

> The idea of a calling or vocation is first and foremost about being called by God, to serve Him within his world. Work was thus seen as an activity by which Christians could deepen their faith, leading it on to new qualities of commitment to God. Activity within the world, motivated, informed, and sanctioned by Christian faith, was the supreme means by which the believer could demonstrate his or her commitment and thankfulness to God. To do anything for God, and to do it well, was the fundamental hallmark of authentic Christian faith. Diligence and dedication in one's everyday life are, Calvin thought, a proper response to God.[94]

Calvin challenged believers "to work, to perform, to develop, to progress, to change, to choose, to be active, and to overcome until the day of their death or the return of their Lord."[95] Calvin encouraged believers to be involved as salt and light in the world. "For Calvin, it is entirely possible to maintain integrity of faith while injecting a Christian presence and influence within society."[96]

Calvin also believed in the personal pervasiveness of God's sovereignty, which made a profound difference in his approach to vocational calling. Calvin understood Scripture to teach that "the whole of a man's life is to be lived as in the Divine Presence."[97] Four hundred years later Abraham Kuyper concluded that "It is from this mother-thought that the all-embracing life system of Calvinism sprang."[98] As John Piper explains:

> Calvin's doctrine of "vocation" follows from the fact that every person, great and small, lives "in the Divine Presence." God's sovereign purposes govern the simplest occupation. He attends to everyone's work. This yielded the Protestant work ethic. Huge benefits flow from a cultural shift in which all work is done earnestly and honestly with an eye to God.[99]

Contemporary Biblical scholars have expressed the concern that if we equate *talents* with gifts and abilities throughout Jesus' parable, the conclusion is difficult to justify. "For example, the first two servants double their 'talents;' this implies that using one's gifts and abilities will result in the gaining of more gifts and abilities rather than improving the gifts and abilities one already has which is the usual understanding."[100] Additional difficulties arise when the one talent of the lazy servant is taken away and given to the first servant. It is unclear how that part of the parable could refer to gifts and abilities.

As we have suggested, the term *talent* in the sense of mental endowment or natural ability was derived from this parable. The word was first used in this way in the English language during the 1430s.[101] Taking nothing away from Calvin, we should be careful not to read our current meaning of the word *talent* back into the parable.

Taking this caution into account, many contemporary Biblical scholars have expanded on Calvin's definition. Craig Blomberg identifies the talents as a portion of God's resources.[102] I. H. Jones suggests we should consider whatever endowment a Christian may have received.[103] Brad H. Young includes everything that a person has, whether goods or abilities.[104] John B. Carpenter gives a more open interpretation: "Parables are about principles, and this parable is about faithfulness of endeavor."[105] Carpenter goes on to say that the money was used as an example of everything with which we have been endowed by God and that we cannot identify the talents more specifically.[106] R. T. France offers this opinion: "In the context of Jesus' ministry the sums of money entrusted to the slaves are more likely to represent not natural endowments given to men in general, but the specific privileges and opportunities of the kingdom of heaven . . . to be faithfully exploited before the master returns."[107] Similarly, John Paul Heil argues that the talents are "a rather general and open-ended symbol of all that Jesus has entrusted to his disciples for promoting the reign of the heavens during the time between his resurrection and final coming."[108]

One of the most interesting definitions of *talent* comes from Ben Chenoweth, who writes:

> Matthew intended the talents to refer to "the knowledge of the secrets of the kingdom of heaven."

> In other words, the disciples have been given inside information about the kingdom—they were given the interpretation of Jesus' parables unlike the crowds who only heard the parables—and therefore they must make use of this knowledge to bring about a profit for Jesus.[109]

Don Carson agrees that we cannot pin down the precise meaning of *talent:* "Attempts to identify the talents with spiritual gifts, the law, natural endowments, the gospel, or whatever else, lead to a narrowing of the parable with which Jesus would have been uncomfortable. Perhaps he chose the talent or mina symbolism because of its capacity for varied application."[110]

In the most general sense, we can conclude that the *talents* are "creational, deriving from the creative activity of God, who invites us through their use to be co-creators with God to make God's world work and to build up the body of Christ."[111] They are the tools God gives us to carry out the Cultural Mandate. And in this context we can be assured that whatever the Lord gives us now He will ask us about later, expecting us to diligently work with these resources for the furtherance of His Kingdom.[112]

The Parable of the Talents teaches us that God gives us everything we need in order to do what He has asked us to do. The apostle Paul saw himself as responsible to God for what had been entrusted to him:

> So then, men ought to regard us as servants of Christ and as those entrusted with the secret things of God. Now it is required that those who have been given a trust must prove faithful. I care very little if I am

judged by you or by any human court; indeed, I do not even judge myself. My conscience is clear, but that does not make me innocent. It is the Lord who judges me. Therefore judge nothing before the appointed time; wait till the Lord comes. He will bring to light what is hidden in darkness and will expose the motives of men's hearts. At that time each will receive his praise from God. (1 Corinthians 4:1-5)

In the Garden of Eden, Adam was given resources to take dominion and produce a return on God's investment. Likewise all Christians are "enjoined to participate in ways framed by the revelation of God's work in the creative and renewing work of world-making and remaking. And it is in the divine nature of this work that vocation is imbued with great dignity."[113]

The master expects His servants to do more than passively preserve what has been entrusted to us. He expects us to generate a return by using our talents toward productive ends. The servant who received five talents had everything necessary to produce five more; the servant who received two had everything necessary to produce two more; and the servant who received one had everything necessary to produce one more.

Calvin and the Reformers also taught that our talents are given not merely for our personal joy but for the common good. The Puritan William Perkins defined *calling* as a "certain kind of life, ordained and imposed on man by God, for the common good."[114] This is why the master rewards the two faithful servants with invitations to share the master's happiness (Matthew 25:21, 23).

According to the Scriptures, Christians will be held accountable not only for how we have loved our neighbor (Matthew 25:31-46) but for what we have done with our talents (Matthew 25:14-30). Scripture also teaches us that one of the primary ways we glorify God and love our neighbor is through our vocational calling to work.[115]

There was once a young man who was very gifted at teaching God's Word. He saw teaching the Bible as his vocational calling, and he studied diligently, teaching at every opportunity, working tirelessly to increase the effectiveness of his craft. He believed that if he worked hard enough, one day he would be the "best in the world." He would be the next Billy Graham or R.C. Sproul. Many years passed, and although he was well received and valued wherever he taught, he began to have doubts that he would ever reach his goal to be the "best in the world." One day, reading the Parable of the Talents, he had an epiphany. He realized that he was a two-talent servant, while the Billy Grahams and R.C. Sprouls of the world are five-talent servants. As a two-talent servant, he was never going to be the "best in the world." This revelation should have been devastating, but it was not, because he saw in the parable another great truth. The reward for the faithful servant with two talents was the same as the reward for the faithful servant with five talents. The reward of entering into the Master's joy was based on being faithful with what God had given him. If he was faithful, his reward would be to enter into the joy of Master. That reward is the same for all who faithfully serve Christ, regardless of the level of gifts that have been given to them. He finally realized that he had to define *success* in Biblical terms rather than as the world had taught him.

There is a poignant scene in the 1981 Academy Award-winning movie *Chariots of Fire*. Eric Liddell, a devout Scottish Christian, is preparing to run in the 1924 Olympics. Liddell's athletic success has made him a celebrity. His sister believes that Eric's popularity has caused him to forget his promise to return to China as a missionary. Liddell assures her that he will return to China, but first he must run in the Olympic Games. He believes that God made him for a purpose, but God also made him fast. When he runs, Liddell says, he feels God's pleasure.

Certainly Eric Liddell was a five-talent servant, but all of us should feel God's pleasure when we are faithful to our calling. This is especially true regarding our vocational calling. We know that we work in a fallen world. Because of the curse of sin, our work will be difficult, and we will not feel God's pleasure all the time or at the level we will enjoy in the world to come. But we should feel satisfaction and joy from doing our best with what God has given us in the place where His providence puts us.

Cornelius Plantinga, in his book *Engaging God's World*, points out a potential pitfall of this view of success. He writes that those who attempt to change the world in a big way run the risk of oscillating between pride and despair, between thinking that they have the magic solution that will eliminate the problem in a generation and thinking that the problem will never go away, no matter what they do.[116] He goes on to offer the following solution:

> So, on one hand, we don't need to take responsibility for trying to fix everything. The earth is the Lord's, and he will save it. On the other hand, we take responsibility for contributing what we uniquely have to contribute to the Kingdom, joining with many others from across the world who are striving to be faithful, to add the work of their hands and minds to the eventual triumph of God.[117]

The 16th century French mathematician and philosopher Blaise Pascal said that the Christian gospel replaces pride with humility and despair with hope, and nowhere is this more desperately needed than in the work of our vocational calling.[118]

Reading Matthew's interpretation of Jesus' Parable of the Talents presents us with a challenge. If one has been entrusted with the knowledge of the secrets of the Kingdom of Heaven—and anyone who has read Matthew's Gospel is given that very knowledge—then one is expected to put that knowledge to good use. Those who make increase will be praised with the words, "Well done, good and faithful servant . . . . Enter into the joy of your master" (Matthew 25:21 ESV). Those who fail to make any increase will be punished with the words, "You wicked, lazy servant!" (Matthew 25:26). It is up to us which response of the Master we will receive.[119] Our work is to be driven by our love of the Master, and our only desire should be to receive His praise.

If these five foundational ideas about work, The Four-Chapter Gospel, The Cultural Mandate, The Kingdom of God, Common Grace and the biblical Meaning of Success are true, why has the Church not taken them more seriously? The answer to this question can be found in the next chapter.

Chapter 3

The History of Work and Calling

This is what the LORD says: "Stand at the crossroads and look; ask for the ancient paths, ask where the good way is, and walk in it, and you will find rest for your souls."

—Jeremiah 6:16

Why does today's church have such a distorted view of work? If we look back over the last 2000 years of Christian history, we discover that the idea of *vocation* has been understood quite differently at various times. Prior to the Christian era we find two sharply contrasting views of everyday work among the Greeks and the Jews.

The Greek View of Work

During New Testament times, Roman and Greek attitudes about work were shaped by Aristotle, who taught that it was demoralizing and demeaning to work with your hands or to work for pay. For example, he wrote: "The object which a man sets before him makes a great difference; if he does or learns anything for his own sake or for the sake of his friends, or with a view to excellence, that action will not appear illiberal; but if done for the sake of others, the very same action will be thought menial and servile."[120]

Aristotle said that to be unemployed was good fortune, because it allowed a person to participate in the life of contemplation. He argued that the contemplative life is the happiest life.[121] Greek society was organized so that a few could enjoy the blessings of leisure while work was done by those in lower social-economic positions and slaves.

The Hebrew View of Work

Although the Jews also valued the opportunity to think about issues and engage in contemplation, they held a different view of work. The Old Testament placed a high value on work, even menial labor. Work was part of God's purposes in creation. Theological reflection would be done by people who were also daily engaged in everyday life in the world. It is significant to note that Jewish teachers, unlike their Greek counterparts, were not expected to live off the contributions of their students, but were expected to have a trade to support themselves.

Saul of Tarsus (who would become the Apostle Paul) was a perfect example of the Jewish idea of work in the first century A.D. He was a Roman citizen, which afforded him a somewhat privileged social status with respect to laws, property, and governance. He was the brilliant student of Gamaliel the Elder, considered one of the leading Jewish minds of his time. Yet Saul would have been expected to learn a trade to support himself. In his case, he learned to be a tentmaker.

The Early Christian View of Work

In light of the Old Testament background, it is not surprising to see the same appreciation of work in the first-century Christian church. Though He called his disciples out of their vocations, Jesus gave no general call for all Christians to give up everyday work. Much of His teaching drew on themes from the world of everyday work, with no self-consciousness or apologies.

Paul also emphasized a positive view of work when he commanded all Christians to continue in their work and to work well (Colossians 3:23-24; 1 Thessalonians 4:11-12). Paul continued in his trade as a tentmaker during his church planting ministry (Acts 18:3).

Continuing in their everyday occupations was apparently the general Christian pattern for the first century after the Apostles. Christians gave glory to God in and through their occupations. They did the same jobs as unbelievers, but they did those jobs in a distinctly Christian way. In the Letter to Diognetus from the second century A.D. we read this description of the everyday lives of Christians:

> For Christians cannot be distinguished from the rest of the human race by country or language or customs. They do not live in cities of their own; they do not use a peculiar form of speech; they do not follow an eccentric manner of life. This doctrine of theirs has not been discovered by the ingenuity of deep thought of inquisitive men, nor do they put forward a merely human teaching, as some people do. Yet, although they live in Greek and barbarian cities alike, as each man's lot has been cast, and follow the customs of the country in clothing and food and other matters of daily living, at the same time they give proof

of the remarkable and admittedly extraordinary constitution of their own commonwealth. They live in their own countries, but only as aliens. They have a share in everything as citizens, and endure everything as foreigners. Every foreign land is their fatherland, and yet for them every fatherland is a foreign country. They marry, like everyone else, and they beget children, but they do not cast out their offspring. They share their board with each other, but not their marriage bed. It is true that they are "in the flesh," but they do not live "according to the flesh." They busy themselves on earth, but their citizenship is in heaven. They obey the established laws, but in their own lives they go far beyond what the laws require . . . . What the soul is to the body that the Christians are to the world.[122]

By the ordinariness and yet the distinctiveness of how they lived, the early believers invited their pagan neighbors, by word and witness, to consider the truth of the faith they proclaimed. Although there is no specific mention of occupations in the Letter to Diognetus, it is clear that the early Christians had a sense of vocational calling. The picture we see through the eyes of this second-century writer is of Christians working out their holiness in the ordinary callings of their lives. They were truly salt and light in their culture. As a result, they radically changed their world in the first few centuries after the death and resurrection of Christ.

By the beginning of the third century we begin to see a subtle shift in the way Christians understood vocation. Conflicts with Jew and pagans gave rise to persecution, which led Christians to see themselves at war with the surrounding culture. They worshipped a different God, lived by a different law, had a different inward character and therefore saw the world as simply wicked. In this light Tertullian argued that Christians could not participate in the military, in politics, or in trade with the world. "After we become Christians," Tertullian said, "we have no need of Greek philosophy." Jerusalem and Athens have nothing to do with one another.[123]

By the end of the third century, with the end of persecution, the separation between Jerusalem and Athens began to disappear. The Church Fathers began to be more heavily influenced by Greek thought. In their theology, the positive view of all work as God's work began to change to the Greek view that work is demeaning. We can see this influence in the writings of Eusebius and Augustine.

Eusebius of Caesarea writes of two contrasting ways to live. There is the "perfect life," the *vita contemplativa,* consisting of sacred vocations dedicated to contemplation; this life is reserved for priests, monks, nuns, and those in similar religious orders. Then there is the "permitted life," the *vita activa,* which encompasses secular vocations dedicated to action, such as governing, farming, trading, soldiering, and homemaking.[124]

Eusebius the perfect Christian life was one devoted to serving God untainted by physical labor. Those who chose to work (or had to work) for a living were second-class Christians. Here we see the beginnings of the early monastic tradition, which would fully develop in the medieval church during the Middle Ages.

In a similar way, Augustine distinguished between the *active life* and the *contemplative life.* While both kinds of life were good—Augustine had praise for the work of farmers, craftsmen, and merchants—the contemplative life was of a higher order. At times it might be necessary to follow the active life, but wherever possible, one should choose the other: "The one life is loved, the other endured."[125]

The church not only embraced Augustine's view but expanded it to the point that it dominated Christian thinking until the Reformation. The duality between the spiritual and secular was being established. Pursuing the contemplative life or a professional role in the church would soon be the only truly religious vocation.

The Medieval Church's View of Work

The sacred-secular divide produced the mistaken belief that work had less value than contemplation in God's Kingdom. Until the Reformation, this error shaped much subsequent Christian thinking regarding vocation. "By the time Christianity became the official religion of the Roman Empire, the distinction between clergy and laity was fairly well established. With the establishment of celibacy for the clergy in the 11th century, this demarcation was complete and the laity were relegated to second-class status in the church."[126] This trend was also reinforced by the rise of monastic spirituality, which regarded vocation as a calling out of the world into isolation in the desert or the monastery.

In the medieval church, having a *vocation* or *calling* referred exclusively to full-time church work. If a person felt a calling, this was a sign that he or she might "have a vocation," which meant becoming a priest, a monk, or a nun. The ordinary occupations of life—being a peasant farmer or kitchen maid, making tools or clothing, being a soldier or even king—were acknowledged as necessary but worldly. Such people could be saved, but they were mired in the world. To serve God whole-heartedly and to live a genuinely spiritual life required a full-time commitment. The "counsels of perfection" could be fulfilled only in the Holy Orders of the church, in which a man or woman devoted every day to prayer, contemplation, worship, and the service of God. Even marriage and parenthood, though recognized as good things, were viewed as encumbrances to the religious life. "Having a vocation" included the willingness and the ability to live a celibate life.[127]

The division of life into sacred and secular categories during the Middle Ages, with the subsequent subordination of the laity to the professional priesthood, marginalized the New Testament view of the priesthood of all believers. This point was not lost on Martin Luther.

The Reformation View of Work

It was initially through Martin Luther's efforts that the 16th century Reformers began to recover the Biblical doctrine of work. They began to recognize that all of life, including daily work, can be understood as a calling from God. In an amazing statement for his time, Luther wrote in *The Babylonian Captivity of the Church:*

> Therefore I advise no one to enter any religious order or the priesthood, indeed, I advise everyone against it—unless he is forearmed with this knowledge and understands that the works of monks and priests, however holy and arduous they may be, do not differ one whit in the sight of God from the works of the rustic laborer in the field or the woman going about her household tasks, but that all works are measured before God by faith alone.[128]

Luther led the Reformers to sharply contrast the monastic call "from the world" with the authentically Christian call "into the world."

In *The Fabric of This World*, Lee Hardy summarizes Luther's position on *vocation:* "Vocation is the specific call to love one's neighbor." According to Luther, we respond to the call to love our neighbor by fulfilling the duties associated with our everyday work.[129] This work includes domestic and civic duties as well as our employment. In fact, Luther said we can only truly serve God in the midst of everyday circumstances, and all attempts to elevate the significance of the contemplative life are false.[130]

Thirty years after Luther, second generation Reformer John Calvin developed an even more dynamic view of *calling* which encouraged a greater degree of urban enterprise and the possibility of changing vocations. Alister McGrath explains, "Theology for Calvin offered a framework for engaging with public life." Calvin taught that every believer has a vocational calling to serve God in the world in every sphere of human existence, lending a new dignity and meaning to ordinary work.

> Underlying this new attitude is the notion of the vocation or "calling." God calls his people, not just to faith, but to express that faith in quite definite areas of life . . . . Luther and Calvin regarded vocation as a calling into the everyday world. The idea of a calling or vocation is first and foremost about being called by God, to serve Him within his world. Work was thus seen as an activity by which Christians could deepen their faith, leading it on to new qualities of commitment to God. Activity within

the world, motivated, informed, and sanctioned by
Christian faith, was the supreme means by which the
believer could demonstrate his or her commitment
and thankfulness to God. To do anything for God,
and to do it well, was the fundamental hallmark of
authentic Christian faith. Diligence and dedication
in one's everyday life are, Calvin thought, a proper
response to God.[131]

Calvin's view of vocation is less static than Luther's, encouraging
a greater degree of self-consciousness to examine possibilities and
the potential to change occupations. At the time such a change was a
revolutionary idea. Some historians would even say that John Calvin
himself laid the foundation for today's market-based economy.[132]
Calvin wrote, "We know that people were created for the express
purpose of being employed in labor of various kinds, and that no
sacrifice is more pleasing to God than when every person applies
diligently to his or her own calling, and endeavors to live in such a
manner as to contribute to the general advantage."[133]

Calvin called believers to become salt in the world, introducing a
Christian presence and influence within the world in which they lived.
This vision of a Christian society was very appealing to Calvin's
followers, particularly the Puritans. John Winthrop (1588-1649), one
of the leaders of the Massachusetts Bay Colony, envisioned a Christian
civilization in the New World based on Calvin's understanding of the
Scriptures. In a sermon to the Massachusetts Bay colonists aboard
the ship *Arbella,* Winthrop predicted that their new community
would be a city upon a hill, watched by the world.

The Reformed view of work and calling was further developed
by the Puritans, who also encouraged enterprise and thrift. They

maintained a strong ethic which emphasized stewardship and service. "Puritan religion reflected Calvin's zeal for embodying faith in society and culture. The Piety of the Puritans was not individualistic. Like Calvin, they believed that Christians were called upon to build a community of faith that would transform the world."[134] But what is known as the Protestant Work Ethic would be overtaken by the Enlightenment and then by the Industrial Revolution.

The 18th and 19th Century View of Work

During the 17th and 18th centuries, a wide-ranging intellectual movement called the Enlightenment emerged. The goal of the Enlightenment was to understand the natural world and humankind's place in it solely on the basis of reason, without turning to religious belief.

Immanuel Kant was the last influential Enlightenment philosopher of modern Europe, and his thinking continues to influence Western thought into the 21st century.[135] Kant's ideas opened the way for a radical change in society's prevailing view of work.

Kant divided reality into two parts, the *phenomenal* and the *noumenal*. The phenomenal is the public world of empirical fact, that which can be proven with reason alone. Once something is proven, you can know it for certain, and you can publicly encourage others to believe it. By contrast, the noumenal world deals with morality and spirituality, things which cannot be rationally or empirically proven. All beliefs in this realm must be accepted by faith; therefore we cannot know these things for certain. Noumenal beliefs should be kept private and outside the public domain.

Such a dichotomy between fact and spirit produced a pronounced compartmentalization in Western thinking. Sacred and secular are seen as divided, which leads to an incorrect understanding of vocation as being strictly secular. As an accommodation to Kantian philosophy, theological liberals such as Friedrich Schleiermacher reduced the Christian faith to a system of ethics, downgrading the idea that Christians are to live the totality of our lives to God.

Also during the first half of the 19th century, there was a fundamental shift in the theology and practice of American evangelicalism. Preachers such as Charles Finney led a revival movement which has come to be known as the Second Great Awakening. Although it was part of a larger movement which opposed Enlightenment ideas, the movement was focused on obtaining professions of faith. The revivalists' techniques were pragmatic, and in the process they affirmed the "spiritual" over and against the "secular." For American Christians, the legacy of this movement has been an increased dichotomy between work and faith.

During this same time period, two additional forces emerged which would have lasting influence on the theology of work in the Western world: the industrial revolution and Marxism. Some historians argue that the Protestant work ethic ushered in the "spirit of capitalism," which led to the industrial revolution.[136] Others maintain that the historical shift resulted from a corruption of the Protestant work ethic and the effects of the Enlightenment.

Regardless of the origin of the idea, the concept of *vocation* became so closely associated with a person's *career* that the words became synonymous, and all connection with the calling of God disappeared. The views of vocation held by the Reformers and Puritans failed to address the rapid changes brought on by industrialization.

While Marxism and capitalism are regarded as opposites, both see the pursuit of a vocation as an end in itself. Both encourage workers to look for personal fulfillment through the labor of their own hands. Where once the medieval church threatened to divorce faith from work, now work has become an idol to which we look for our identity.[137]

What Karl Marx promised the alienated workers of mid-19th century England was that the work of their hands mattered to history. While he profoundly misread the human heart, he did speak to the deep human longing that we all hunger for our work to matter. The hammer and sickle, ordinary tools, represent the hope that what one does day after day will affect history and that the world will be different because of what we do.[138]

Neither capitalism nor Marxism can deliver on the promise to bring significant meaning to our work. That is why so few people, including Christians, find genuine satisfaction in their jobs.

As a result of these sociological changes and the theological shift brought about by the Second Great Awakening, by the end of the 19th century the Biblical doctrine of work was all but lost to the church.

It is said that history repeats itself because so many people do not pay attention the first time. That proves true in the area of integrating faith and work. Although the early church had a sound Biblical understanding of work, cracks began to form as writers such as Augustine, influenced by Greek thought, began to say that Christians were to serve in the world *when necessary.* The distortion came to full bloom by the Middle Ages with the Catholic Church's separation of faith and work. The Reformers brought back a Biblical understanding of calling and vocation, only for the concept to be lost again during the Enlightenment and Industrial Revolution.

Today the church needs to embrace the truth of the Biblical doctrine of work. It is one of the most important gifts God has given us to influence the world and to find deep satisfaction in our lives here and now. "What does the worker gain from his toil? . . . I know that there is nothing better for men than to be happy and do good while they live. That everyone may eat and drink, and find satisfaction in all his toil—this is the gift of God" (Ecclesiastes 3:9, 12-13).

CHAPTER 4

Our Current Situation

God himself will milk the cows through him whose
vocation that is. He who engages in the lowliness
of his work performs God's work, be he lad or
king. [139]

—Martin Luther

In her most recent book, Laura L. Nash, senior research fellow at the
Harvard Business School, states that many Christian businesspeople
experience a "radical disconnection between Sunday services and
Monday morning activities, describing a sense of living in two
worlds that never touch each other."[140]

Nash suggests that these disconnected businesspeople receive
little or no help from their pastors and clergy. She has found "a seismic
difference in their worldview about the meaning of capitalism and
profit. For the clergy, profit was a clear sign of 'me-first' self-interest,
materialism and therefore not Christian. To the businessperson, profit
was a result of actions that were partially others-oriented combined

70

with a legitimate pursuit of self-interest, such as serving a customer, creating jobs, or donating part of the proceeds to charity."[141]

The disconnect between business and clergy probably explains the experience of William Diehl, a former Bethlehem Steel executive:

> In the almost thirty years of my professional career, my church has never once suggested that there be any type of accounting of my on-the-job ministry to others. My church has never once offered to improve those skills, which could make me a better minister, nor has it ever asked if I needed any kind of support in what I was doing. There has never been an inquiry into the types of ethical decisions I must face, or whether I seek to communicate my faith to my coworkers. I have never been in a congregation where there was any type of public affirmation of a ministry in my career. In short, I must conclude that my church doesn't have the least interest whether or how I minister in my daily work.[142]

Mr. Diehl is left with the same frustration which nags at many Christian businesspeople today. They feel they are in a support position for others who are "in the ministry," and though they play an important role, they are not really where the action is for God's Kingdom.[143]

The integration of faith and work is misunderstood not only by the church members who sit in the pews but by those who stand behind the pulpit. Our vocation should be "an element of Christian discipleship; a habit of the mind and heart of listening for and responding to the voice of the Lord,"[144] yet this concept is missing from most churches.

At the beginning of the 21st century we are confronted with a wall between personal faith and public work. The wall has been raised by two distortions of the purpose of our work. Os Guinness calls them the two "grand distortions:" the "Catholic Distortion" which elevates the spiritual at the expense of the secular and the "Protestant Distortion" which elevates the secular at the expense of the sacred.[145]

"Did you hear Joe Smith has left his job at the bank to go into fulltime Christian service as a pastor?" That would be an example of the Catholic Distortion, which devalues vocational work in the eyes of God. It misapplies the apostle Paul's references to his work of tentmaking (Acts 18:1-3; 20:33-35). For example a person in business might say, "I see my job as tentmaking, it provides for my family, but what I do that's really important to God is my work as a lay leader in the church and my charitable work with other non-profit organizations." As we have seen, Paul would have held a firmly Jewish outlook on his vocational work. He would have seen it not as a means to an end, but as important to God in its own right.

In contrast to the Catholic Distortion, the Protestant Distortion of work is a form of dualism. It does not elevate the secular at the expense of the spiritual; rather it severs the secular from the spiritual altogether.[146] It turns work, a good thing, into an idol, an ultimate thing. Tim Keller defines an *idol* as "anything more important to you than God, anything that absorbs your heart and imagination more than God, anything you seek to give you what only God can give."[147] Keller goes on to write:

> We know that a good thing has become a counterfeit
> god when its demands on you exceed proper
> boundaries. Making an idol out of work may mean
> that you work until you ruin your health or you
> break the laws in order to get ahead . . . . Idolatry is
> not just a failure to obey God, it is a setting of the
> whole heart on something beside God.[148]

When we are introduced to someone, what is one of the first things we ask? "What do you do?" We mean, "What is your job?" In our contemporary society, we define ourselves by career. Even most Christians find their identities in their vocational pursuits. Our work no longer serves God; instead, it serves ourselves. "As a secular perversion of calling, careerism invites people to seek financial success, security, access to power and privilege, and the guarantee of leisure, satisfaction and prestige."[149]

To avoid both the Protestant Distortion and the Catholic Distortion requires a successful integration of faith and work. Evangelical Christians fall far short in that area.

Yet there is hope. Many Christians today earnestly desire a deeper, more integrated approach to serving God in their work. They are looking for an approach that takes into account the Christian as a whole person, not a life compartmentalized and divided by conflicting demands of different roles. They want to be men and women who serve God with heart, soul, and mind in every sphere of life, as husband or wife, parent, church member, employer, or employee.[150]

Many Christians today continue to struggle with understanding how to integrate a holistic understanding of work into their daily lives. In order to move away from these two distortions and begin to see work in the proper perspective, we must first understand the difference between *calling* and *work*.

The Difference Between Calling and Work

Harvard Business School psychologist Timothy Butler offers the following advice about how *vocation* differs from *career* or *job:*

> There are three words that tend to be used interchangeably—and shouldn't be. They are "vocation," "career," and "job." Vocation is the most profound of the three, and it has to do with your calling. It's what you're doing in life that makes a difference for you, that builds meaning for you, that you can look back on in your later years to see the impact you've made on the world. A calling is something you have to listen for. You don't hear it once and then immediately recognize it. You've got to attune yourself to the message.[151]

The Christian community today has the same difficulty understanding the differences between *vocation, career,* and *job.* To complicate matters further, we throw in the word *calling,* which may or may not mean the same thing as *vocation.* In order to understand God's vocational call on our lives, we need to grasp how these words relate to each other and how they are used in the Scriptures.

If we look at the origins of the words *career* and *vocation,* we immediately get a feel for the difference between them. *Vocation* comes from the Latin verb *vocare,* which means "to call," which explains why Timothy Butler equates *vocation* and *calling.* The definition suggests that a person listens for something which calls out to him. The calling is something which comes to someone and is particular to someone. Today this terminology is used only when we refer to someone going into some type of religious service. John feels that he is called to become a pastor. For the rest of us *vocation* refers only to a particular occupation, business, or profession.

In the secular world, *career* is the term we most often hear regarding work. The word *career* originates from the medieval Latin noun *carraria,* which means "a road for vehicles." It is fitting that we commonly use the term *career path.* A career is usually associated with a certain occupation. Becoming a lawyer or a securities analyst is a *career* choice; however it is usually not the same as a calling.

The most specific and immediate of the three terms is *job.* It has to do with current employment and a specific job description. These days, it is difficult if not impossible to try to describe what someone's job will be twelve months from now.

Primary and Secondary Callings

The doctrine of *vocation* was developed with its greatest rigor by Luther, Calvin, and the other Reformers. They believed that our first call is to follow Jesus out of darkness into light and out of death into life. This principal calling includes a call to faith in Christ (Romans 8:28-30; 1 Corinthians 1:9), a call to the Kingdom of God (1 Thessalonians 2:10-12), a call to eternal life (1 Timothy 6:12; Hebrews 9:15), and a call to holy living (1 Corinthians 1:2; 1 Peter 1:15). As we have already mentioned, this is what Os Guinness call our *primary calling.*

The Reformers also recognized something else called *vocational calling,* which is the call to God's service in one's work. This is one of what Os Guinness calls our *secondary callings.* There are additional secondary callings in different realms, such as family, society, and church.[152]

Our obedience to our *primary calling* to Christ can be seen working itself out in these four *secondary callings,* which are the call to human family, the call to church, the call to community, and the call to vocation. (see figure 1)

One of our *secondary callings* is to be a part of our human family: brother, sister, son, daughter, father, or mother. God established marriage in the Garden and told Adam and Eve to be fruitful and multiply, which implies families. The family is one of the ways we are to fill the world with the image of God and thus fulfill part of the Cultural Mandate.

Another *secondary calling* is to the church. All members of the church possess spiritual gifts, natural gifts, and abilities. We are called to use our gifts in service within the church to build up the body of Christ, to strengthen the body, and to carry out its purpose within the world. The diversity of gifts, each supporting the other, strengthens the whole church "until we all reach unity in the faith and in the knowledge of the Son of God and become mature, attaining to the whole measure of the fullness of Christ" (Ephesians 4:13).

The third *secondary calling* which flows from our primary calling was described by the Puritan author William Perkins as "a certain kind of life ordained and imposed on man by God for the common good."[153] The gospel commands us to serve God's purposes in the world through civic, social, political, domestic, and ecclesiastical roles. We are to love God and to love our neighbor in the larger community beyond the church by engaging in justice and mercy as God leads us. Tim Keller in his book *Ministries of Mercy* insists, "To say that evangelism can be done without also doing social concern is to forget that our goal is not individual 'decisions,' but the bringing of all life and creation under the lordship of Christ, the kingdom of God."[154]

Finally the fourth *secondary calling* which follows from our primary calling is our call to vocational work. We may also term it our *vocational calling.* The work of believers possesses a significance which goes far beyond the visible results of that work. The process of doing the work, as much as the results of the work, is significant to God. There is no distinction between spiritual and temporal, sacred and secular. All human work, however lowly, is capable of glorifying God. Work is the potentially productive act of praise. Work glorifies God, it serves the common good, and it is something through which human creativity expresses itself.[155]

Throughout this book we will use the term *vocational calling* in the same way as the Reformers. We will affirm that a Christian's work is not a specific type of occupation but rather an attitude that sees work "not, primarily as a thing one does to live, but the thing one lives to do . . . . [Work] is, or it should be, the full expression of the worker's gifts, the thing in which he finds spiritual, mental and bodily satisfaction, and the medium in which he offers himself to God."[156] Under this definition you may have different careers and jobs at different points in your life, but your *vocational calling* from God will stay constant.

A Shift in the Meaning of Calling

Vocational calling in the medieval church applied only to the holy orders of the priests. Not until the Reformation do we see the idea of vocational calling applied to all work. In regard to the secondary calling of vocation, Martin Luther wrote:

What you do in your house is worth as much as if you did it up in heaven for our Lord God. For what we do in our calling here on earth in accordance with His word and command He counts as if it were done in Heaven for Him . . . . Therefore we should accustom ourselves to think of our position and work as sacred and well-pleasing to God, not on account of the position and the work, but on account of the word and faith from which the obedience and the work flow.[157]

Fifty years later, Puritan author William Perkins wrote in his *Treatise of the Vocations or Callings of Men*:

Every person of every degree, state, sex, or condition without exception must have some personal and particular calling to walk in. The main end of our lives . . . is to serve God in the serving of men in the works of our callings . . . . the true end of our lives is to do service to God in serving of man.[158]

In order to understand the Biblical doctrine of work, we must clearly understand the differences between *vocational calling* and career, occupation, or job. *Vocational calling* is the call to God and to His service in the vocational sphere of life based on giftedness, desires, affirmations, and human need. *Vocational calling* is usually stable and permanent over a lifetime. Discovering our vocational calling is possible because it is based on giftedness, interests, passions, and human need, which are all easy to identify. Frederick Buechner in his book *Wishful Thinking* put it this way: "The place

God calls you to is the place where your deep gladness and the world's deep hunger meet."[159]

A career should be based on the opportunities for service which are presented to a believer enabling him or her to fulfill their *vocational calling*. Finding the right occupation at any one time is a matter of God's specific leadership, guidance, and provision. Solomon wrote, "A man can do nothing better than to eat and drink and find satisfaction in all his work. This too, I see, is from the hand of God, for without Him, who can eat or find enjoyment?" (Ecclesiastes 2:24-25).

Our *vocational calling* from God to the workplace is something above a job or even a career. Out of the primary calling of God flow secondary calls to action in certain areas of our lives. Luther and the other Reformers "extended the concept of divine call, vocation, to all worthy occupations."[160] They saw occupation as timely opportunity for service, in God's providence, presented to believers to enable them to fulfill their vocational calling through what we would call everyday work. Rather than equate *vocational calling* with a specific occupation or career, we are called to be Christians in whatever situations we find ourselves.[161] "So whether you eat or drink or whatever you do," Paul urged the Corinthians, "do it all for the glory of God" (1 Corinthians 10:31).

Vocational calling stays the same as we move in and out of different jobs and careers. Our *vocational calling* is directly related to the discovery of our God-given talents. Over time we develop and hone them into useful competencies for the glory of God and the service of others, often in various jobs and occupations. "The New Testament treats work in the context of a larger framework: the call of God to live totally for him and his kingdom."[162]

Yet work is about more than us and God; it unites us within community. Work makes us interdependent. Work cultivates the resources of the material and human universe. Work is the form in which we make ourselves useful to others; civilization is the form in which others make themselves useful to us. Work unifies the human race and carries out the will of God.[163]

With this in mind, how do we then define *work* from a Biblical perspective? John Stott defined work as "the expenditure of energy (manual or mental or both) in the service of others, which brings fulfillment to the worker, benefit to the community and glory to God."[164] Dorothy Sayers gave us a more detailed description when she said that work should be seen:

> . . . not as a necessary drudgery to be undergone for
> the purpose of making money, but as a way of life
> in which the nature of man should find its proper
> exercise and delight and so fulfill itself to the glory
> of God. That it should, in fact, be thought of as a
> creative activity undertaken for the love of the work
> itself; and that man, made in God's image, should
> make things, as God makes them, for the sake of
> doing well a thing that is well worth doing.[165]

Through our faithful labor we imitate God's own creativity, order, and appreciation for beauty and excellence. The Reformers clearly understood this, and as a result the Protestant church during the Reformation enjoyed its greatest cultural influence, seen in art, literature, music, and the social institutions of their day. Recovering the Biblical doctrine of work can open the way for contemporary Christians to influence their culture in the same way.[166]

A clue for how we can revive the neglected Biblical doctrine of work is found in Francis Schaeffer's prophetic work *A Christian Manifesto*. In the 1980s Schaeffer wrote this about the United States:

> The basic problem of Christians in this country . . . in regard to society and in regard to government is that they have seen things in bits and piece instead of totals. They have very gradually become disturbed over permissiveness, pornography, the public schools, the breakdown of the family, and finally abortion. But they have not seen this as a totality— each thing being a part, a symptom, of a much larger problem. They have failed to see that all of this has come about due to a shift in worldview—that is, through a fundamental change in the overall way people think and view the world and life as a whole. This shift has been away from a worldview that was at least vaguely Christian in people's memory toward something completely different.[167]

The Reformers radically changed their world in a couple of generations by bringing Christians back to the Biblical understanding of work as part of a larger all-encompassing Biblical worldview. As Christians today, we have similar possibilities. To be salt and light in this world, we must commit ourselves to a worldview which sees our place in God's Kingdom in the context of all redemptive history.

This is a vision which sees our work as important to God and as a gift from God, bestowed on us to influence the world for His glory and the furtherance of His Kingdom. "The obvious implication is that the new humanity (God's people) is called to promote renewal in every department of creation . . . . We have a redemptive task wherever our vocation places us in his world."[168] In order to take advantage of our opportunity to further the Kingdom in the here and now through our vocational calling, we must rediscover the Biblical doctrine of work, confident that it is the most powerful tool God has given us to have an impact on this present world.

CHAPTER 5

The Future:
Work, Calling, and Cultural Renewal

May the favor of the Lord our God rest upon us;
establish the work of our hands for us—
yes, establish the work of our hands.

—Psalm 90:17

There is an old story set in the Middle Ages during the construction of one of the great European cathedrals. A nobleman was walking among the workers, asking about their labors. The stonemason explained the care involved in raising a plumb wall. The glass worker pointed out the details of a leaded glass window. The carpenter spoke about the wooden frame which provided the support for the whole building. Finally the nobleman spotted a peasant woman with a broom and a bucket going around cleaning up trash. He asked her what she was doing. She replied, "I'm building a cathedral for the glory of God!"

The peasant woman had a firm grasp on what we have called the Biblical doctrine of work.

What are the implications of the Biblical doctrine of work for Christians today?

First, we must rediscover that our primary call is to follow Jesus. We must realize that this call encompasses the whole of our lives, including our everyday work. Our call should lead Christians to a radically different lifestyle, seeking not to follow the culture but to influence the culture for the glory of God. If we live in light of the two great commandments, to love God and our neighbor, our lives will be nothing short of radically countercultural. Following Christ whole-heartedly will have a transformational effect on all of life, including our vocational calling.

We must see every part of our life—work, civic, family, recreational, church—as a living sacrifice to God (Romans 12:1) and do everything to the glory of God (1 Corinthians 10:31). We cannot confine our spiritual life to the weekend and conduct our business in the world with the same values and attitudes as everyone else. We must ask questions such as: "If my work is important to God, how should I be conducting my business? How should I be spending my money? How should I live in my neighborhood and municipality? How should I be acting and living in this area of my life?"[169] The answers to these questions will help us successfully integrate the life of faith with work.

Second, we must understand the mission that we have been called to do in this world. If we were created to work, what should our work look like? We must recognize the tension present in the Scriptures regarding work. For the Christian, life without work is meaningless; but work must never become the meaning of one's life. We must find our identity in Christ, not in our work. It is our union with Christ which transforms our hearts and gives us the desire to serve Him out of gratitude while we engage the world.

Finally, we must realize that the purpose of our work is to have an impact on culture with the ultimate goal to redeem culture. A prominent metaphor in the Bible is the bringing of light into a dark world (Matthew 5:16; John 1:5). When light is brought into a dark room, the room is transformed. The light of the gospel has the power to radically transform individual people and their culture as a whole.

The Biblical doctrine of work is one of the most powerful means God provides for us to shape and influence culture. Yet today we hear many Christians say that we should *not* be involved in shaping culture. People who say this are actually supporting the social status quo, whether they agree with it or not. Tim Keller had this to say in a recent essay on work and culture:

> When Christians work in the world, they will either assimilate into their culture and support the status quo or they will be agents of change. This is especially true in the area of work. Every culture works on the basis of a "map" of what is considered most important. If God and his grace are not at the center of a culture, then other things will be substituted as ultimate values. So every vocational field is distorted by idolatry.[170]

When Christians do their jobs with excellence and with accountability, in a distinctively Christian manner, they cannot help but have a profound effect on the world around them. Thomas Cahill, in his book *How the Irish Saved Civilization*, tells how Christian monks in the Middle Ages moved out of Ireland and through pagan Europe. Along the way they invented and established academies, universities, and hospitals. Through these new institutions the monks transformed local economies and cared for the unfortunate.[171]

The Irish monks' goal was not to change the pagan culture into the church. Instead, their vocation was inspired by the gospel, and that changed the way they carried out their work. They worked for the flourishing of all mankind rather than strictly for themselves.

Christians today have a similar opportunity. If we are serious about the truth of Christianity, we need to engage in cultural renewal, working to serve the common good toward the furtherance of the Kingdom and for the glory of God.

Our Calling to Be Obedient Servants

Walk onto almost any Christian college campus and you can hear these ideas being taught: Christians should challenge their spheres of influence with Christian truth claims. God wants us to bring all areas of thought and life under the captivity of the Lordship of Christ (2 Corinthians 10:5). To accomplish this, we need to develop a distinctly Christian worldview. A *Christian worldview* means that a Christian thinks God's thoughts after Him in every discipline of study, whether in art, science, history, psychology, or economics, then applies his or her learning on the canvas, in the laboratory, at the chalkboard, in the counseling process, or in the business world.[172]

Even though the necessity of a Christian worldview has been taught for years, today our surrounding culture has more influence on the church than the church has on our surrounding culture. Worldview teaching is not translating into real observable change. A recent Barna survey found that only 19% of professing born-again Christians acknowledged even a limited Christian worldview (based on Barna's definition). That figure has remained unchanged for the past 13 years.[173]

Two problems are obvious here. First, only a minority of evangelical Christians hold to a truly Biblical worldview. Second, those who do are not making much of an impact.

In 1999, Charles Colson and Nancy Pearcey reintroduced a new generation to the concept of Christian worldview in their book *How Now Shall We Live?*, a follow-up to Francis Schaeffer's *How Should We Then Live?* Colson and Pearcey wrote that our lives and work have been separated from their original mission because Christians have lost the concept of a Biblical worldview. The central premise of the book is that a comprehensive Christian worldview is necessary for Christians to successfully engage and influence their culture.

Since Colson and Pearcey's book was published, Christian worldview studies have exploded. There are hundreds of books, classes, and websites dedicated to the concept of Christian worldview. For example, a Google search of "Christian worldview" returns over 736,000 results. So why is all this education having so little effect?

Something vital is missing. A review of current Christian worldview teaching exposes the absence of a vital New Testament concept: the idea of *sacrifice*.

The Scripture verse quoted most often in worldview studies is Romans 12:2: "Do not conform any longer to the pattern of this world, but be transformed by the renewing of your mind. Then you will be able to test and approve what God's will is—his good, pleasing and perfect will." Yet verses one and two are meant to be read together, because in the original Greek they are all one sentence. The lead-in to verse 2 is Romans 12:1: "Therefore, I urge you, brothers, in view of God's mercy, to offer your bodies as living sacrifices, holy and pleasing to God—this is your spiritual act of worship."

The Christian worldview has the power to impact culture only when we put these two verses together and read them as Paul intended. The intellectual renewal of verse two is important, but the power to live a life that makes a difference comes only from a commitment to deny ourselves and take up our cross daily to follow Jesus (Luke 9:23).

Dietrich Bonhoeffer wrote in a letter, "The religious act is always something partial; faith is something whole, involving the whole of one's life. Jesus calls us not to a new religion, but to life."[174] Those who are called by Christ are no longer their own; they are "bought with a price" (1 Corinthians 6:19-20). Bonhoeffer also memorably wrote, "When Christ calls a man, he bids him come and die."[175] The death may not be physical (although that may be required), but it is always the death of the self to the will of God. Those called must be willing to persevere until the end in the labor to which they have been called.

In 1559, John Calvin began a seminary in Geneva to train young church planters. We know that Calvin sent at least 88 church planters to his native country of France, possibly many more.[176] It was dangerous to plant churches in France because of anti-Protestant sentiment. In fact it was so dangerous that the Academy of Geneva became known as "Calvin's School of Death" because so many graduates went out to martyrdom.[177] If any of our seminaries today were nicknamed "The School of Death," they would be empty!

Many contemporary Christians who have supposedly been taught a Christian worldview continue to buy into one of the great secular lies of our culture: "You can have it all." They believe they have the right to have any job they choose and live a prosperous lifestyle with all the indulgences, and as long as they do a Bible study at work and attend church, they have fulfilled their Christian obligations.

While there is nothing intrinsically wrong with being financially successful, as long as we seek to fulfill our vocational calling, we must be willing to sacrifice what *we want* for what *God wants*, laying down our personal choices for what God has chosen for us. For some of us, that might mean turning down a job on Wall Street to do relief work in Haiti. For others, it might mean turning down a job doing relief work in Haiti to work on Wall Street. Unlike the rich young ruler who came to Jesus (Luke 18:18-23), we need to be willing to give our lives as a living sacrifice out of gratitude for what Christ has done for us. That is what the apostle Paul urges us to do in Romans 12:1-2.

A genuinely Christian worldview is more than an intellectual collection of philosophical and religious beliefs. If it is going to affect the way we live, it must embrace both our minds and our hearts. It means "living as an obedient Christian in all of life—heart, mind, fingers, and toes."[178] As Paul told servants in the Colossian church, "Whatever you do, work at it with all your heart, as working for the Lord, not for men, since you know that you will receive an inheritance from the Lord as a reward. It is the Lord Christ you are serving" (Colossians 3:23-24). Brian Walsh and Richard Middleton offer further explanation:

> All we do is to be done from a heart filled with love for God. If our lives are not an expression of our love for him, they will express rebellion against him. That is simply our religious nature as God's image bearers. All our cultural life is subject to Yahweh's norms, and we are called to respond to him in obedience.[179]

Our vocational call flows out of a sacrificially committed life transformed by the power of the gospel of Jesus Christ. Here in the United States, however, we have made Christianity too easy. We have taught a so-called Christian worldview which requires little or no sacrifice from us. What is the answer to this dilemma?

In a 2006 article in *Christianity Today* titled "Young, Restless, Reformed," Collin Hansen noted that under the radar there has been a quiet and steady growth of interest in traditional Reformed theology. "While the Emergent 'conversation' gets a lot of press for its appeal to the young, the new Reformed movement may be a larger and more pervasive phenomenon."[180] The contemporary Reformed revival has grown out of a reaction against anti-intellectual Christianity, with its over-emphasis on personal experience. It longs for a robust and coherent theology which engages believers to live sacrificially in all spheres of life.

As we saw in the example of "Calvin's School of Death," the Reformation Christian worldview acknowledges the importance of sacrifice. Calvin himself wrote in his *Institutes:*

> We are not our own: let not our reason nor our will, therefore, sway our plans and deeds. We are not our own: let us therefore not set it as our goal to seek what is expedient for us according to the flesh. We are not our own: in so far as we can, let us therefore forget ourselves and all that is ours. Conversely, we are God's: let us therefore live for him and die for him. We are God's: let his wisdom and will therefore rule all our actions. We are God's: let all the parts of our life accordingly strive toward him as our only lawful goal.[181]

For Calvin these were not empty words. He meant them in an intense and personal way. In 1538, after he had spent two shaky years as pastor in Geneva, the General Assembly ordered him to leave the city within three days. Calvin went to Strasbourg to take up his new position as minister to French refugees. In Strasbourg, Calvin's ministry prospered, and his church grew to 400-500. In 1541 the Geneva Council requested Calvin to return to Geneva. Calvin was emotionally torn; he wanted to stay in Strasbourg, yet he wanted to be faithful to God's call in his life. He wrote to a friend, "When I received that letter, I would have rather died than go back to Geneva, but I am not my own. I belong to God and therefore that is where I am going."[182]

An authentic Biblical worldview does more than avoid the artificial religious/secular division of life; it motivates us to be willing to sacrifice ourselves for the gospel of Jesus Christ. The only appropriate response to the free gift of salvation is obedience to God's call in every area of life.

Our Calling to Reweave Shalom

Imagine an enormous tent city on the edge of the greatest metropolis in the world. The refugees who live here have been forcibly taken from their homeland by an invading army. They have seen their city sacked, their families murdered, and their sacred place of worship destroyed. They are bitter toward their captors and would rise up and break free if they could. This is the scene of the Israelites living in exile in Babylon in the 6th century B.C.

One day a letter is brought to the exiles from their homeland. It is from the prophet Jeremiah, who was left behind in Jerusalem. The letter radically changes the Jewish people's perception of how they should live in this alien land. Part of the letter reads:

> This is what the LORD Almighty, the God of Israel, says to all those I carried into exile from Jerusalem to Babylon: "Build houses and settle down; plant gardens and eat what they produce. Marry and have sons and daughters; find wives for your sons and give your daughters in marriage, so that they too may have sons and daughters. Increase in number there; do not decrease. Also, seek the peace and prosperity of the city to which I have carried you into exile. Pray to the LORD for it, because if it prospers, you too will prosper (Jeremiah 29:4-7).

The key phrase in this short passage from the book of Jeremiah is "seek the peace and prosperity of the city." The word used for *peace* is the Hebrew word *shalom,* which has a far more comprehensive meaning than the English word *peace.* Cornelius Plantinga explains *shalom* as:

> . . . the webbing together of God, humans, and all creation in justice, fulfillment, and delight . . . Shalom means universal flourishing, wholeness and delight—a rich state of affairs in which natural needs are satisfied and natural gifts fruitfully employed, a state of affairs that inspires joyful wonder as its Creator and Savior opens doors and welcomes the creatures in whom he delights. Shalom, in other words, is the way things ought to be.[183]

In the Garden of Eden before the Fall, there was perfect shalom. There was universal flourishing, and things were the way they were supposed to be. Man's fall into sin had a devastating effect on the whole of creation. It was as if the very fabric of the created order began to unravel, and the whole creation began to experience a lack of shalom.

Shalom bookends human existence. It characterizes the Garden (the way it was supposed to be) and the eternal City (the way it is going to be), and so provides the vision for our existence in between.[184]

In the tent city in Babylon, a young man in the crowd heard Jeremiah's letter and believed that it meant a new vocational call on his life. From that moment, he totally committed his life to working for the *shalom,* the peace and well-being, of the great city of Babylon. The young man's name was Daniel.

We can find no better model for vocational calling in the Old Testament than the story of God's call on Daniel's life. Like Daniel and the other Hebrew exiles, we are strangers in a strange land. If we take our Christian worldview seriously, we will find ourselves at odds with much of the surrounding culture, just as Daniel found himself. Yet like Daniel we must not withdraw from the world in which we live, but rather engage it in obedience to God's call on our lives.

Daniel's approach to life in Babylon as a public servant meant that he sought to use his gifts through his vocational calling to transform the culture around him. He wanted Babylonian life be shaped by the values of the one true God, not by prevailing pagan values. At the same time, he worked for the flourishing of all of Babylon.

Daniel was able to identify the shared ground where his values and Babylonian values overlapped. Through Daniel's conscientious work, his Babylonian overlords became convinced of the excellence of Daniel's vision of their shared future.

There was a limit, however, to what Daniel was willing to do. When his government demanded ultimate loyalty, he refused, choosing instead what appeared to be certain death in the lion's den. God saved Daniel and continued to use him as a great witness within the Babylonian Empire.

In Jeremiah's letter to the Babylonian exiles, he is reminding them of the "Cultural Mandate." He tells them to, "Build houses and settle down; plant gardens and eat what they produce. Marry and have sons and daughters; find wives for your sons and give your daughters in marriage, so that they too may have sons and daughters. Increase in number there; do not decrease." In other words, to be fruitful and multiply, fill this part of the world to which he has brought them with His images. Second, He tells them to, "seek the peace and prosperity of the city to which I have carried you into exile." This is what taking dominion should look like for the exiles. For them taking dominion is reweaving Shalom. Jeremiah has given us a big picture of not only what the exiles vocational calling looked like but ours as well. David Dark in his book Everyday Apocalypse says it this way:

> The movement called Christianity . . . cannot be understood apart from the Jewish concept of shalom. The Christian gospel does not call people to give their mental assent to a certain list of correct propositions, nor does it provide its adherents with a password that will gain them disembodied bliss when they die and the pleasure of confidently awaiting their escape until then. Shalom is a way of being in the world. The Christian gospel invites us to partake in shalom, to embody shalom, and to

anticipate its full realization in the coming kingdom
of God.[185]

Jeremiah's message to the exiled people of Israel was simple.
God meant them to be a blessing to the world even while they lived
in Babylon. God intends the same for us. We are called to work
for the shalom of the city, whatever or wherever that city is, where
God has put us. We are to be a blessing in our time and place. This
is possible only because we have found our identity in Christ, the
Prince of Shalom. Because of Him we know what real shalom is
supposed to be.

Like Daniel, we have a decision to make. Will we join those who
conform, or those who renew and transform? Will we, like Daniel,
embrace our Biblical call to vocation to become agents of shalom,
models of shalom, and witnesses to shalom?[186]

We will never create full shalom in this current age. Such
fulfillment awaits the age to come, when Jesus will establish
everlasting shalom in the New Heaven and the New Earth. Still,
like the exiles in Babylon, we can build toward that future. The
work we do in the here and now is important to God and serves as a
signpost to point others to the New City, the City of God, where all
of God's children will live one day in perfect shalom. Until then our
calling is to work for the shalom of this present world to the glory
of God, by the grace of God reweaving the unraveled fabric of our
broken world.

Our Calling to Restore Culture

If a significant part of our calling as God's people is to reweave
shalom, what will that look like in our world today? As we have
already seen, God's Cultural Mandate demands that Christians

embrace their responsibility to influence the greater culture through the most powerful means at their disposal—their vocational calling. As Henry Blackaby says, every Christian should "watch to see where God is at work and join him."[187]

When Christians work to serve the common good of their neighbors, we generate unparalleled influence on the culture.[188] Culture "in the broadest sense is the purpose for which God created man after His image . . . . God's image had been granted to man so that he might in his dominion over the whole earth bring it into manifestation. And this dominion of the earth includes not only the most ancient callings of men, such as hunting and fishing, agriculture and stock-raising, but also trade and commerce, finance and credit, the exploitation of mines and mountains, and science and art. Such culture does not have its end in man, but in man who is the image of God and who stamps the imprint of his spirit upon all that he does, it returns to God, who is the First and the Last."[189]

Today we do not see the imprint of God being stamped on the prevailing human culture to any great extent. Instead, as Tim Keller observes:

> When many Christians enter a vocational field, either they seal off their faith and go to work like everyone else around them, or they spout Bible verses to their coworkers. We do not know very well how to persuade people of Christianity's answers by showing them the faith-based, worldview roots of everyone's work. We do not know how to equip our people to think out the implications of the gospel for art, business, government, journalism, entertainment, and scholarship.[190]

Now we arrive at two important questions. First, should Christians try to influence culture at all? Second, why have Christian attempts been so ineffective in influencing culture?

For centuries, Christians have struggled to articulate an effective Biblical position regarding the church's interaction with culture. In his classic 1951 book *Christ and Culture*,[191] which is still influential today, H. Richard Niebuhr suggested five potential methods of modeling the interface between Christ and culture. Although Niebuhr's theology is not always evangelical, his insights remain helpful as we think through the issues of cultural engagement.

The first alternative is "Christ Against Culture," which encourages opposition, total separation, and hostility toward culture and a commitment to creating a separate, pure community (that is, culture) of Christians. Tertullian, Tolstoy, Menno Simons, and in the 20th century, Jacques Ellul are exponents of this position. The Amish, Mennonites, and Anabaptists have their roots in an oppositional stance between Christianity and culture. This group tends to culturally withdraw from the world, either trying their best to ignore it or providing negative criticism from a safe moral distance.

The second alternative is the "Christ of Culture." It is exactly the opposite of "Christ Against Culture" because it attempts to bring culture and Christianity together, regardless of their differences. Liberation, process, and feminist theologies are recent examples. "Liberal" Protestantism would fit into this category.

The third alternative is "Christ Above Culture." This position attempts "to correlate the fundamental questions of the culture with the answer of Christian revelation."[192] Thomas Aquinas is the most prominent teacher of this viewpoint. It is embraced by both the Roman Catholic and the Eastern Orthodox Churches.

The fourth alternative is "Christ and Culture in Paradox." In this viewpoint, the Christian belongs "to two realms (the spiritual and temporal) and must live in the tension of fulfilling responsibilities to both."[193] Martin Luther adopted this view. He reasoned that a person experiences Christ through simultaneous interaction between two kingdoms.

The fifth and final alternative is "Christ the Transformer of Culture." Proponents of this view include the "conversionists" who attempt "to convert the values and goals of secular culture into the service of the kingdom of God."[194] Augustine, Calvin, John Wesley, Jonathan Edwards, John Knox, Ulrich Zwingli, Abraham Kuyper and Francis Schaeffer are the chief proponents of this last view.

While Niebuhr's model is not a perfected system, it shows the multiple perspectives of how Christians throughout history have related to their surrounding cultures. Many current evangelical Christians throughout the United States would be found in the "Christ Against Culture" camp. This explains the reluctance of many to engage today's culture.

The Reformed tradition has historically embraced "Christ the Transformer of Culture." We can trace this perspective from John Calvin through the Dutch theologian and politician Abraham Kuyper to contemporary thinkers such as Francis Schaeffer and Al Wolters. This perspective embraces the idea that creation is inherently good; therefore human culture is not to be despised but should be celebrated and developed because it is part of God's intent for the human race.

We are to be actively involved in the transformation of culture without giving culture undue prominence. "If you want to make a powerful and lasting impact on the culture, you've got to do more than just consume it, critique it, condemn it, or copy it. The only way to truly change the culture is to create something new for it—

something that will inspire people enough to start to reshape their world."[195]

The idea of *Christ transforming culture* takes seriously the overall Biblical narrative of creation, fall, redemption, and restoration. It celebrates the goodness of creation and therefore of human culture. It recognizes the fallenness of creation, but it also recognizes God's desire to restore creation by the death and resurrection of Christ, through the ministry of the church.

To the first question, "Should Christians try to influence culture at all?" we would answer in the affirmative. The Bible calls us to engage, redeem, and restore culture; this is at the very heart of the Cultural Mandate.

This brings us to our second question: Why have Christian attempts been so ineffective in influencing culture? James Davison Hunter suggests that Christians generally employ three failed tactics to try to bring about cultural change: 1. Evangelism: not only as a way of saving souls but of transforming individuals and, indirectly, the culture; 2. Political Action: elect Christians who have the right values and worldview and therefore will make the right choices; 3. Social Reform: renew civil society through social movements of moral reform (addressing problems within families, schools, neighborhoods, etc.)

Hunter argues none of those three tactics can change the world, because flawed presuppositions underlie their strategies. The foremost error, Hunter says, is the idea that the essence of culture is found in the hearts and minds of *individuals*. According to Hunter, social science and history prove that popular ideas such as "transformed people transform cultures" and "in one generation, you change the whole culture" fail to work because they do not take into effect the power institutions play in forming and maintaining culture.[196]

Hunter further explains, "Evangelism, political action, and social reform are worthy undertakings, but they aren't decisively important if the goal is world changing. These strategies don't attend to the institutional dynamics of culture formation and cultural change; in fact, they move in exactly the opposite direction of the ways in which cultures do change."[197] Hunter sums up his argument in the following statement:

> In terms of the cultural economy . . . Christians in America today have institutional strength and vitality in the lower and peripheral areas of cultural production . . . . The main reason why Christian believers today (from various communities) have not had the influence in the culture to which they have aspired is not that they don't believe enough, or try hard enough, or care enough, or think Christianly enough, or have the right worldview, but rather because they have been absent from the areas in which the greatest influence in the culture is exerted. The culture producing institutions of historical Christianity are largely marginalized in the economy of culture formation in North America. Its cultural capital is greatest where leverage in the larger culture is weakest.[198]

While Hunter's argument helps explain the weakness of Christian impact on American culture over the last 100 years, it fails to acknowledge the centuries of positive influence Christianity has exerted over Western civilization. Sociologist Rodney Stark stresses in his book *The Rise of Christianity* that Christianity's 40% growth per decade during the first three centuries A.D. can be credited to Christians' deep involvement in the fabric of their culture:

> Christianity served as a revitalization movement that arose in response to the misery, chaos, fear and brutality of life in the urban Greco-Roman world . . . . Christianity revitalized life in Greco-Roman cities by providing new norms and new kinds of social relationships able to cope with many urgent problems. To cities filled with the homeless and impoverished, Christianity offered charity as well as hope. To cites filled with newcomers and strangers, Christianity offered an immediate basis for attachment. To cities filled with orphans and widows, Christianity provided a new and expanded sense of family. To cities torn by violent ethnic strife, Christianity offered a new basis for social solidarity. And to cities faced with epidemics, fire, and earthquakes, Christianity offered effective nursing services . . . . For what they brought was not simply an urban movement, but a new culture capable of making life in Greco-Roman cities tolerable.[199]

D. James Kennedy and Jerry Newcombe's book *What If Jesus Had Never Been Born?* details the profound impact of the Christian religion, and specifically Calvinism, upon the culture of the Western world.[200] They demonstrate that "Christians, for distinctively Christian motives, have vastly influenced western culture in such areas as help for the poor, teaching of literacy, education for all, political freedom, economic freedom, science, medicine, the family, the arts, the sanctity of life."[201]

The Bible itself is responsible for much of the language, literature, and fine arts we enjoy today. Christian artists and composers through the centuries have been heavily influenced by the Bible, and their work reflects its influence. Contrary to many history texts' treatment of the subject, Christian influence on values, beliefs, and practices in Western culture are abundant and well-ingrained into the flourishing society of today.[202]

Nowhere is the cultural influence of Christianity more apparent than in the history of the United States. The Puritan John Winthrop proclaimed in a 1630 sermon that their new community would be a city upon a hill, watched by the world. Until the beginning of the 20th century, American evangelicals enjoyed a position of cultural dominance. "But after the Scopes trial and the rise of theological modernism, religious conservatives turned in on themselves. They circled the wagons, developed a fortress mentality and championed separatism as a positive strategy."[203]

We have already seen a number of the historical and theological reasons for American Christians' cultural retreat, including the two-chapter gospel, the influence of Enlightenment thinking, and the Industrial Revolution. Yet the most overlooked reason for the failure of the church to influence the culture is the loss of the Biblical doctrine of work. T.M. Moore suggests that our vocational calling is inseparably linked to our interaction with and our impact on the surrounding culture:

> So the creation has been "subjected to futility,"
> Paul says, and we who have become the sons and
> daughters of God, who understand His purpose for

our work, have been called in our work to repair, renew, and restore the original beauty, goodness, and truth of God . . . . Our work only takes on full significance when we see it in this light, as part of God's ongoing work to bring everything to a higher state of goodness (Romans 8:28). So no matter what your job, or whatever your work might be, God intends that you should devote your labors to something greater than personal interest, economic prosperity, social good, or future beneficence alone. God intends your work to contribute to the restoration of the creation, and the people in it, to raising life on this blue planet to higher states of beauty, goodness, and truth, reflecting the glory of God in our midst. We will only fully appreciate the value and potential of our work when we see it in that light.[204]

God changes culture through Christians' faithful participation in our vocational calling. This has been the primary instrument which God has used over the ages to change culture. James Davison Hunter is correct when he says that "Cultures are shaped when networks of leaders, representing the different social institutions of a culture, work together towards a common goal. Again and again we see that the impetus, energy and direction for changing the world were found where cultural, economic and often political resources overlapped; where networks of elites, who generated these various resources, come together in common purpose."[205] The *elites*, as Hunter calls them, are engaged in their own vocational callings; Christians must do the same if we want to once again make a difference in our world.

Christians cannot simply rest satisfied with individual conversions or separated enclaves when they discern the central plot-line of the Bible: A) God created a world of peace and life; B) the world has fallen into a state of injustice and brokenness; C) God has determined to redeem this world through the work of His Son and the creation of a new humanity; until D) eventually the world is renewed and restored to being the world that God made and that we all want. In short, the purpose of redemption is not to help individuals escape the world. It is about the coming of God's Kingdom to renew the world. God's purpose is not only saved individuals, but also a new world based on justice, peace, and love, rather than power, strife, and selfishness. If God is so committed to this purpose that He suffered and died, surely Christians should also seek a society based on God's peace and love.[206]

Theologian Donald Bloesch says that culture "is the task appointed to humans to realize their destiny in the world in service to the glory of God."[207] The Cultural Mandate calls us to fill the world with the images of God (evangelism) and to take dominion (redeeming culture); it is not *either/or* but *both/and.* "If you lose the emphasis on conversion, on 'my chains fell off, my heart was free, I rose, went forth, and followed thee' [quoting Charles Wesley's hymn *And Can It Be]*—you will lose the power of the gospel for personal transformation. You will not have people who will work sacrificially, joyfully, and non-paternalistically for justice. If you lose the emphasis on the corporate—on the kingdom—you lose the power of the gospel for cultural transformation."[208]

Gabe Lyons captures the heart of many Christians when he says, "I can't imagine anything more important or significant in our lifetime, than to be a part of the church recapturing its role in shaping culture. When we do this, the life-giving message of Jesus Christ will go forward in ways unprecedented throughout the 21st century."[209] Motivated by the Cultural Mandate and inspired by the power of the gospel of Jesus Christ, through our vocational calling we have the opportunity to transform our communities, our nation, and the world. Our effectiveness will provide a catalyst for sustained cultural renewal.

> God's people can, as agents of His redemptive plan, transform business, stripping it of selfish ambition and pursuing instead what's best for their neighbors. Through business, God's people can harness mankind's creativity, and with it nurture His creation, developing products that make the world more satisfying. Through the economic power of commerce, Christians can make the world safer and healthier. The members of Christ's Church, distributed in offices around the world, can transform greed into good stewardship, showing the world that business has a biblical responsibility to create new wealth and provide a fair return to investors (Matthew 25:14-28). But, with an eye toward the consummation of Christ's kingdom, we also create wealth in order to create new and satisfying jobs,

which offer the hope (and perhaps a glimpse) of a
coming world where there is no poverty.[210]

If we can restore the Biblical doctrine of work, Christianity can
once again bring its powerful influence to bear on our culture. "As
God's Spirit penetrates people's hearts through the gospel, those
people become new creatures (2 Cor. 5:17). They take their faith into
every sphere of life, including the workplace, politics, economics,
education, and the arts. And in all these realms, they seek to glorify
God. They hear Paul's exhortation in 1 Cor. 10:31, 'whether you
eat or drink, or whatever you do, do all to the glory of God.' They
obey, imperfectly to be sure. But their incipient obedience leads to
significant changes in society."[211]

It has been suggested that cultures are profoundly resistant to
intentional change, and therefore major shifts in culture take place
only over very long periods of time.[212] Yet during the Reformation
a fairly small group of people brought about radical cultural change
within a single generation. More recently, here in the United States,
we have seen another example of major culture transition within a
fairly short period of time. In the late 1980s a group of about 175
leaders meet in Warrington, Virginia, to strategically launch several
initiatives through various channels of cultural influence to support
what they hoped would bring about substantial cultural change. Gabe
Lyons describes what happened next:

> These friends formed the beginnings of the
> homosexual movement and were responsible for
> helping it find its stride in the mid-nineties as every
> channel of culture was systematically inundated
> with the message of equal rights, tolerance and

civility for homosexuals. As Paul Rondeau points out in Selling Homosexuality to America, " . . . their strategy was employed in five important markets of social influence . . . which touch every citizen in America; government, education, organized religion, the media, and the workplace." In the business channel, vigorous attempts were finally successful for same-sex couples to be recognized with benefits equal to married couples. In the education channel, books like, Heather Has Two Mommies and Daddy's Roommate about same-sex parenting found their way into schools and public libraries. In television, Ellen and Will and Grace became the wedge that broke open wide acceptance of gays as fun, engaging, and talented human beings. Later, the Fab Five from Queer Eye for the Straight Guy made television ratings soar by showing that gay men are intelligent, have a sense of humor and should be the authorities on fashion sense, design and trend-setting. Within the cultural channel of the church, major denominations like the Episcopal Church and the United Church of Christ opened leadership roles for gays and lesbians. In thirty years, the idea of being gay had moved from being commonly viewed as abnormal and abhorrent in society, to being an acceptable and normal alternative life-style. This illustrates perfectly the potential for cultural influence to happen when leaders throughout the seven channels of culture work together towards a common goal.[213]

In less than 30 years this group brought about significant cultural change. They were successful because they persuaded the decision makers from the areas in which the greatest influence on the culture is exerted.

Christians are already positioned as leaders and decision makers within many of the institutions necessary to establish sustained cultural renewal. They already have authority in the areas in which the greatest influence on the culture is exerted. Yet they are ineffective because they see no connection between what they do on Sunday and what they do on Monday. They are physically present but not spiritually present. They do not understand that the most powerful tool God has given them to impact the world around them is their vocational work. As we see in the example above, profound change is very possible in our present culture. Until Christians embrace the Biblical doctrine of work, they will remain ineffective, because they will continue to practice a separation of faith and work which leaves them helpless to impact the culture around them for the glory of God and the furtherance of His Kingdom.

CHAPTER 6

Conclusion:
How Then Should We Work?

I undertook great projects: I built houses for myself
and planted vineyards . . . . I bought male and female
slaves . . . . I also owned more herds and flocks than
anyone in Jerusalem before me. I amassed silver
and gold for myself, and the treasure of kings and
provinces . . . . Yet when I surveyed all that my
hands had done and what I had toiled to achieve,
everything was meaningless, a chasing after the
wind; nothing was gained under the sun.

—Ecclesiastes 2:4-11

The secular scaled-down version of Solomon's lifestyle shows up in
the modern bumper sticker: "He who dies with the most toys wins."
Even for many Christians, the acquisition of material things and the

pursuit of pleasure are the driving force and measuring rod of what it means to live a successful life.

At the close of the twentieth century, during the height of rampant materialism, work was seen only as a means to an end. Today many people are coming to understand the futility expressed by King Solomon: "Yet when I surveyed all that my hands had done and what I had toiled to achieve, everything was meaningless, a chasing after the wind."

Such demoralizing futility is hitting people at an earlier age. Google "quarter-life-crisis" and you will get over one and a half million hits about young people, usually in their mid—to late 20s, who are unsatisfied with the direction of their lives. These overachievers diligently worked at getting superior grades in high school so they could get into the right colleges and in turn get the best jobs. Now that they are out in the workforce, many are filled with feelings of anxiety and failure. They realize that the world of work is not giving them the satisfaction they expected. One anonymous twenty-something wrote, "You look at your job. It is not even close to what you thought you would be doing or maybe you are looking for one and realizing that you are going to have to start at the bottom and are scared."

Richard Leider and David Shapiro, in their book *Repacking Your Bags: Lighten Your Load for the Rest of Your Life*, found that most people's number-one fear is having lived a meaningless life.[214] According to a recent Harris Poll, a monumental 97% of Generation Y (twenty-somethings) are looking for work which allows them to have an impact on the world.[215] Yet it is a difficult task to find meaning in the current postmodern culture. Douglas Groothuis in his book *Truth Decay: Defending Christianity Against the Challenges of Postmodernism* writes about the contemporary mood:

The self becomes saturated, sated with possibilities, options, and preferences—yet without an inner gyroscope for direction, correction, and inspiration. When all values are constructed, no hierarchy of objective values is possible, no guiding ideal is available, and no taboos intrude; there are only experiments, amusements, and diversions. The postmodern self is protean and dynamic, but also fragmented and ultimately empty of objective meaning. The self was made for better things.[216]

In such a toxic cultural environment, Christians are also at risk. We need to know who we are and whom we serve. We should be crystal clear not only in our theology of salvation but in our theology of work in the Kingdom, finding our identities firmly in the transcendent reality of the triune God. "The Gospel, you see, is not only a message for individuals, telling them how to avoid God's wrath. It is also a message about a Kingdom, a society, a new community, a new covenant, a new family, a new nation, a new way of life, and, therefore, a new culture. God calls us to build a city of God, a New Jerusalem."[217] Again Groothuis observes:

While postmodernists madly "reinvent" themselves (to no ultimate end) ever more rapidly, radically, and frantically, the Christian can rest in his or her identity in Jesus Christ, his Kingdom, and his calling. As we "seek first the Kingdom and its righteousness" (Mt 6:33), our lives are brought into greater harmony with God's truth and, therefore, into greater disharmony with all untruth, postmodernist or otherwise. In so doing, we serve as signs, clues, and rumors of God's objective reality in a world moving toward depravity in nearly every direction.[218]

The separation of faith and calling by Christians through the loss of the Biblical doctrine of work had a devastating effect on the landscape of American culture during the 20th century. As Christians, we are once again called to Biblically integrate our faith and our work, using our vocational calling to influence our communities, our nation, and the world. The theologian Geerhardus Vos described it this way:

> [Christ] cannot be quiet and inactive in us. His kingdom is only fully manifest when we are so governed by His Word and Spirit that we are wholly subject to Him. Christ is the anointed King, not only over His church, but also He has been given to her as Head over all things. Hence, in the activity of believers, by which His rule is realized, lies also the urgency to work in all spheres of life. For the Reformed believer Christianity, by virtue of its covenantal character, is a restless, recreating principle which never withdraws itself from the world, but seeks to conquer it for Christ.[219]

Note the beautiful balance in Vos' words. "Our work is in every sphere of life. We are cultural beings. Yet no work is an end in itself. Our cultural involvements are the reflection of the deeper reality of our relationship with God."[220] When seen from this prospective each one of our vocational callings is Kingdom work.

At the beginning of His ministry Jesus announced, "The time has come. The kingdom of God is near. Repent and believe the good news!" (Mark 1:15). We have already seen how Christians in the last century truncated the four-chapter redemptive story to two chapters, Fall and Redemption, putting the emphasis of the Christian life on salvation. While we do not want to underemphasize the importance of salvation, we must acknowledge that this is not all there is to the gospel. Tim Keller once said, if he had to define the Gospel in a single statement, he might do it like this: "Through the person and work of Jesus Christ, God fully accomplishes salvation for us, rescuing us from judgment for sin into fellowship with him, and then restores the creation in which we can enjoy our new life together with him forever."[221]

Without understanding that Christ died on the cross not only to save us but also to restore all things, Christians get the impression that nothing much about this world matters. Grasping the full implication of the gospel should make Christians interested in both evangelistic conversions as well as service to our neighbor and working for peace and justice in the world.[222] As Christians we must:

> . . . prepare to add one's own contribution to the supreme reformation project, which is God's restoration of all things that have been corrupted by evil. The Old Testament word for this restoration of peace, justice, and harmony is shalom; the New Testament phrase for it is "the coming of the kingdom." You can find the Old Testament's teaching about shalom especially in the prophets, and you can find the New Testament's teaching about the kingdom especially in the Gospels and

in some passages of St. Paul's epistles. According to Scripture, God plans to accomplish this project through Jesus Christ, who started to make "all things new," and who will come again to finish what he started. In the meantime, God's Spirit inspires a worldwide body of people to join this mission of God.[223]

The Kingdom of God is to encompass all spheres of life, especially our work. As agents of that Kingdom, we serve as salt and light wherever the Spirit leads us. "As Christians incarnate their world view in public life they help reverse truth decay in myriad ways. In the midst of the fragmentation of postmodern pluralism, the Christian sees all things as unified in God's overarching plan for the universe, summed up in the supremacy of Christ. All has meaning in reference to that fixed—and living—point (Col 1:15-20; Heb 13:6)."[224]

In spite of the power of the Christian faith to transform the world, many believers complain of the fading influence of Christianity on contemporary culture. Like the author of Psalm 137, they lament:

By the rivers of Babylon we sat and wept
when we remembered Zion.
There on the poplars we hung our harps,
for there our captors asked us for songs,
our tormentors demanded songs of joy;
they said, "Sing us one of the songs of Zion!"

(Psalm 137:1-3)

Disgruntled Christians long for the days when America was a Christian nation. Unfortunately they, like the Psalmist during the exile, have not heard the prophet Jeremiah's challenge to pray and work for the shalom of the city where God has placed them. Each of us individually, and all of us as the church, must embrace our vocational calling, understanding that everything—including our work—matters to God.

In a 2009 interview, the theologian N.T. Wright stressed the lasting impact of what we do for the Kingdom of God:

> What you do in the present matters. It's hard for Protestants to hear that without thinking, "Oh, dear, this is good works again." That's a scare tactic. Sometimes, it's a political scare tactic—to stop Christians from actively working to change the way the world is, confronting [in]justice and building communities of peace and hope instead of ones of violence and hatred. The verse which says it all for me is the last verse in 1 Corinthians [15]. Okay, you've got this great chapter on resurrection. What is Paul going to say after writing a whole chapter on resurrection? Is he going to say, "Since there is a resurrection, spend your time looking up and waiting for this glorious future?" No, he says, "Therefore my beloved ones be steadfast, immovable, always abounding in the work of the Lord, because you know that in the Lord your labor is not in vain." Your work is "not in vain." Why not? Because everything you do in the present, in the power of the Spirit and in union with Christ, everything that flows out of

love and hope and grace and goodness, somehow
will be part of God's eventual Kingdom. That is
the message of the resurrection. The resurrection
is your new body in which you will be gloriously,
truly wonderfully you. The resurrection means
everything you've done in the present through your
body—works of justice and mercy and love and
hope—somehow in ways we don't understand will
be part of God's new creation. We are not building
the Kingdom of God in that old social Gospel sense.
We are building for the Kingdom of God.[225]

Paul Marshall reassures us that our works done for the sake of
the Kingdom of God will have enduring significance:

Our works, here and now, are not all transitory. The
good that we have done will not simply disappear
and be forgotten. This world is not a passing and
futile phase; it will be taken up in God's new world.
Our good buildings, our great inventions, our acts
of healing, our best writings, our creative art, our
finest clothes, our greatest treasures will not simply
pass away. If they represent the finest works of
God's image-bearers, they will adorn the world to
come.[226]

We must be committed to the idea that we express our Christian
discipleship through our employment, which is an important part of
our life in Christ. It is in this realm that we are called to stewardship.
Jesus said, "From everyone who has been given much, much will

be demanded; and from the one who has been entrusted with much, much more will be asked" (Luke 12:48). These are terms of stewardship. As we have already noted, the best commentary on this statement is found in Jesus' parable of the talents (Matthew 25:14-30). This parable tells us that the Master expects us to work while we wait for His return. It also shows us that all we *are* and *have* is a capital investment from the Lord, which we are to invest and return to him with interest.

"There will be an accounting of our blessings. Blessed is the one who can meet that accounting joyfully, but woe to the one who has proven unfaithful." [227] We work hard to produce that return for the Master, not because we fear him, but out of gratitude for what he has done for us.

So then how do we integrate our work and our faith in a way that is pleasing to God?

First, we must rediscover that our primary vocation is the call to follow Jesus. From our primary call flows our call to the church, to the family, to the community, and to economic work. All of life is to be lived under the comprehensive Lordship of Christ (Matthew 28:18).

> We know that men were created for the express purpose of being employed in labor of various kinds, and that no sacrifice is more pleasing to God than when every man applies diligently to his own calling, and endeavors to live in such a manner as to contribute to the general advantage.[228]

We must realize that this call to follow Jesus embraces the whole of our lives, including our everyday work. Our Christian calling finds no separation between the secular and the sacred. To God, what we do on Sunday is no more important or spiritual than what we do on Monday. Everything we do should be unified in obedience to God and for His glory (1 Corinthians 10:31).

We must learn how to think out the implications of the Christian view of reality for the shape of everything we do in our professions. Our theology of work should teach us how to *think Christianly* about all of life, public and private, and about how to work with Christian distinctiveness. In all of our work we must labor as though Jesus Himself is the One we must ultimately please (Colossians 3:17). We must work diligently, ever striving in all our labors to excel still more (1 Thessalonians 4:1). We must also employ good stewardship by using all our gifts and every opportunity to serve the Lord and others (Matthew 25:14-30), setting our minds on our exalted King, who watches over all our labors and takes them even more seriously than we do (Colossians 3:1-3).

We must embrace a view of our vocation which includes some constant elements but is also flexible enough to help us make sense of lives in which the nature and mix of our work is regularly changing. It is projected that college graduates today will not only have a number of jobs during their careers, but will have a number of careers during their lifetimes, some of which have not even been invented yet. Therefore the vocational call will be different for different people, and different at different stages in our lives.

We must be committed to the idea that employment is an important part of life through which we express our Christian discipleship; therefore it must be done with excellence.

Christians need to be practically mentored, placed, and positioned in their vocations in the most advantageous way. They need cooperation with others in the field who can encourage, advise, and advocate for them.

We must realize that through the Christian doctrine of work, God changes the culture. If Christians live in major cultural centers in great numbers and simply do their work in an excellent but distinctive manner, it will naturally produce a different kind of culture than the one in which we now live.

We must identify which cultural practices are *common grace* and can be embraced and which practices are antithetical to the gospel and must be rejected, adapted, or revised for use by believers. This must be done not only for work in general, by also for individual professions such as the arts, law, medicine, and business.

We must call all Christians to rediscover the Cultural Mandate, embracing the opportunity to influence culture to the glory of God and the furtherance of His Kingdom. In the church, we must teach about calling and cultural influence and provide vital support to cultural leaders. "We must become an integral piece of the local culture, convening and encouraging creation of future culture that serves the common good. We must become connoisseurs of good culture, recognizing and celebrating the good, true and beautiful to the glory of God and begin to lead the conversations that will shape future culture."[229]

Finally, we must see our work within the larger perspective of God's plan for the restoration of His creation. In Ecclesiastes, Solomon warned Rehoboam against living "under the sun," holding a vision derived from a purely secular perspective. "If all you can see in your work is what goes on at your work, then you may be stuck in a kind of 'under the roof' perspective that keeps you from envisioning the contribution your work makes to God's larger purposes of beauty, goodness, and truth. With a little imagination, no matter what our job—as long as it is legitimate, and entered into for God's glory (1 Corinthians 10:31)—we can find reasons to praise and thank God for our work and for the way it contributes to restoring uprightness to the world."[230] It is this larger perspective of our daily work which will not only help us see the significance of our labors but will also give us great satisfaction as we embrace what we have called the Biblical doctrine of work.

In 1940 John Gillespie Magee, Jr., a young Christian was one of hundreds of Americans who slipped into Canada to join the Royal Canadian Air Force and to volunteer to fight for Britain against Hitler's war machine. Within a year of his enlisting, Magee was sent to England as a fighter pilot and was assigned to the RCAF No. 412 Fighter Sqaudron, where he rose to the rank of Pilot Officer, flying fighter sweeps and combat missions over France and Britain.

In September 1941, Magee was assigned to test a newer model of the Spitfire V. During one high-altitude test flight that took him to a height of over six miles, he began composing a poem in his mind. After he landed, he sent a short note home to his parents about his experience and included the text of his poem on the back of the letter.

> Oh, I have slipped the surly bonds of earth
> And danced the skies on laughter-silvered wings;
> Sunward I've climbed, and joined the tumbling
>   mirth
> Of sun-split clouds and done a hundred things
> You have not dreamed of—wheeled and soared and
>   swung
> High in the sunlit silence. Hov'ring there,
> I've chased the shouting wind along, and flung

My eager craft through footless halls of air.
Up, up the long, delirious burning blue,
I've topped the windswept heights with easy grace
Where never lark or even eagle flew,
And, while with silent, lifting mind I've trod
The high, untrespassed sanctity of space,
Put out my hand and touched the face of God. [231]

Three months latter he was killed. He was nineteen years old. We may not know John Magee but his poem was made famous by President Reagan in a speech on January 28, 1986 as he consoled the nation after the Challenger space shuttle disaster.

The vocational call on John Magee's life led the eighteen year old to pass up a scholarship to Yale University and instead enlist in the Royal Canadian Air Force. Using his God-given skills he quickly became an accomplished pilot. His poem reveals the great love and satisfaction received from his work as a pilot, even though the hours were long, the working conditions harsh, and the pay substandard. God used the work of this young man's hands every time he climbed into the cockpit of his airplane not only for the common good but also in some small, although significant, way to further God's Kingdom here on earth.

It is easy for us to see how John Magee's work in helping defend Brittan from the assault of the Third Reich served the common good. From our historical perspective, we can also see how God used Magee's vocational calling to impact culture, pushing back the darkness of fascism and positively impacting the Kingdom of God. We have no problem seeing Magee's work as Kingdom work. If Hitler's totalitarianism had not been stopped, religious freedom would have been extinguished in Europe making the spread of the gospel much more difficult. Magee's vocational work is Kingdom work because it serves Christ our king as he establishes "his rule and reign over all creation, defeating the human and angelic evil powers, bringing order to all, enacting justice, and being worshiped as Lord."[232]

What is difficult for many of us to see is how of our own vocational work serves God's Kingdom. All work resulting from our vocational callings has this potential although it is often difficult for us to see specifically what we do day to day as Kingdom work.

As we have seen, the work flowing from God's vocational call on our lives is an extension of God's work of maintaining and providing for His creation. But even more than that, it is reweaving shalom. It is a contribution to what God wants done in the world. It is bringing the reign of God to bear on all of our spheres of influence. It is pushing back the darkness, it is Kingdom work. As we in obedience answer the vocational call in our own lives, we must learn to believe God uses every thing we do. " . . . we know that in all things God works for the good of those who love him, who have been called according to his purpose." (Romans 8:28) *All of our work, even the most mundane things we do are taken by God and transformed into Kingdom work.*

As believers at the beginning of the 21st century, we stand in the same place as the 16th-century Reformers. We have the opportunity to teach the truth of Scripture, including the Biblical doctrine of work, and radically influence our culture, making a positive difference in our communities, our cities, our country, and our world for the glory of God and His Kingdom. "If Christianity is to remain a positive force and influence in American public life, all Christians need to be present within that life, as salt and light. To remain safely behind the barricades may seem more secure, and a lot less risky—but it denies us any chance of reforming, renewing, and recalling our culture. The legacy of John Calvin (and the other reformers) invites us to engage our world, and instructs us in how to do so with integrity."[233]

If we are serious about making a difference, we need to rediscover the Biblical doctrine of work.

About the Author

Hugh Whelchel currently serves as executive director of the Institute for Faith, Work & Economics. This Biblical advocacy think tank is a non-profit, non-partisan, 501(c)(3) organization dedicated to educating and inspiring Christians to embrace a Biblical understanding of faith, work, and economics. In this position Hugh brings a unique combination of senior executive responsibility, creative educational administration, and technical innovation from over thirty years of diverse business experience.

In 2005, Hugh stepped out of a successful business career to share his senior executive experience with Reformed Theological Seminary's Washington DC campus, where he served as Executive Director until 2012. Prior to his time at RTS, he spent fifteen years in the IT industry, helping turn around several regional companies.

In addition to his business acumen, Hugh has a unique passion and expertise in helping individuals integrate their faith and vocational calling. He has served as both the executive director and board member of The Fellows Initiative (TFI), a coalition of Regional Fellows Programs (Post-Graduate Christian Leadership Development Programs) established in key communities around the nation. TFI is an umbrella organization that supports and helps establish new regional Fellows Programs. These comprehensive programs include 3-4 day workplace internships, graduate level academic courses and other activities to help the fellows more fully understand God's vocational calling on their lives as they enter their careers. On this topic, Hugh is frequently called upon to teach and speak at conferences, churches, business groups, and universities around the nation.

A native Floridian, Hugh graduated from the University of Florida and earned a master's degree in theology from Reformed Theological Seminary and moved to Northern Virginia in 2000. Hugh and his wife Leslie now live in Loudoun County, Virginia. As an ordained ruling elder in the Presbyterian Church in America, he serves in leadership at McLean Presbyterian Church in McLean, Virginia and also serves on the boards of several Christian non-profits organizations. In what little spare time he has, Hugh enjoys hiking, golf and restoring old sports cars.

Notes

Chapter 1. Introduction

1. Lisa Cullen, "Three Signs of a Miserable Job," *Time Magazine* <www.workinprogress.blogs.time.com/2007/08/21/three_signs_of_a_miserable_job> (accessed August 21, 2007).

2. Paul Helm, *The Callings: The Gospel in the World* (Edinburgh: Banner of Truth, 1987), 98-99.

3. Abraham Kuyper, *Abraham Kuyper: A Centennial Reader*, ed. James D. Bratt (Grand Rapids: Eerdmans, 1998), 488. Quote from Kuyper's inaugural address at the dedication of the Free University of Amsterdam, October 1880.

4. Dorothy L. Sayers, *Creed or Chaos?* (Manchester, NH: Sophia Institute Press, 1974), 106.

5. Michael P. Schutt, *Redeeming Law:Christian Calling and the Legal Profession* (Downers Grove, IL: InterVarsity Press, 2007), 15.

6. Carl F. H. Henry, *Aspects of Christian Social Ethics* (Grand Rapids, MI: Wm. B. Eerdmans Publishing Co., 1964), 31.

7. Sayers, "Vocation in Work," in *A Christian Basis for the Post-War World*, ed. A. E. Baker (London: Christian Student Movement Press, 1942), 99.

8. Os Guinness, *The Call: Finding and Fulfilling the Central Purpose of Your Life* (Nashville, TN: W Publishing Group, 1998), 4.

Chapter 2. The Gospel, the Kingdom and Our Calling

9. Stuart Briscoe, *Choices for a Lifetime* (Carol Stream, IL: Tyndale House Publishers, 1995), 142.

10. Steve Garber, "Vocation Needs No Justification," *Comment*, Fall 2010.

11. Eugene Peterson, *A Long Obedience in the Same Direction* (Downers Grove, IL: InterVarsity Press, 1980), 104.

12. Os Hillman, International Coalition of Workplace Ministries, Faith and Work Facts and Quotes <www.icwm. net/pages.asp?pageid=203> (accessed May 1, 2010).

13. Michael W. Goheen, "The Urgency of Reading the Bible as One Story in the 21st Century," Public lecture given at Regent College, Vancouver, B.C., Nov. 2, 2006.

14. N.T. Wright, *The New Testament and the People of God* (London: SPCK, 1992), 41-42.

15. Tim Keller, "Our New Global Culture: Ministry In Urban Centers" <www.theresurgence.com/files/Keller%20-%20 Our%20New%20Global%20CultureMinistry%20in%20 Urban%20Centers.pdf> (accessed May 1, 2010).

16. Albert Wolters, *Creation Regained* (Grand Rapids, MI: Wm. B. Eerdmans Publishing Co., 2005), 91.

17. Michael Metzger, "Back and Forth" <www.doggieheadtilt. com/back-and-forth> (accessed May 1, 2010).

18. Chris Wright, *God's Mission: The Key To Unlocking the Bible's Grand Narrative* (Downers Grove, IL: InterVarsity Press, 2006), 66.

19. Wright, *God's Mission,* 24.

20. Goheen, "Urgency."

21. Keller, "New Global Culture."

22. Keller, "Work," Sermon given at Redeemer Presbyterian Church, New York, NY, July 7, 1996.

23. Nancy Pearcey, *Total Truth: Liberating Christianity From Its Cultural Captivity* (Wheaton, IL: Crossway, 2004), 47.

24. Douglas F. Kelly, *Creation and Change* (Ross-shire, Scotland: Mentor, 1997), 224.

25. Richard L Pratt, *Designed for Dignity: What God Has Made it Possible for You to Be* (Phillipsburg, NJ: P&R Publishing, 1993), 20-21.

26. D. James Kennedy, *What If Jesus Had Never Been Born?* (Nashville, TN: Thomas Nelson, 1994), 240.

27. Pratt, *Designed for Dignity,* 7.

28. Pratt, *Designed for Dignity,* 32-33.

29. Pearcey, *Total Truth,* 49.

30. John Frame, "Christianity and Culture," Lectures given at the Pensacola Theological Institute, July 23-27, 2001 <thirdmill.org/magazine/hof/ApolFall2006/Christ%20 and%20Culture.doc> (accessed May 5, 2010).

31. John Frame, *The Doctrine of the Word of God* (Phillipsburg, NJ: P & R Publishing, 2010), 218.

32. John Fesko, *Last Things First: Unlocking Genesis with the Christ of Eschatology* (Fearn, Scotland: Christian Focus Publications, 2007), 167-168.

33. Wolters and Goheen, *Creation Regained: Biblical Basics for a Reformational Worldview* (Grand Rapids, MI: Wm. B. Eerdmans Publishing Co., 1985), 42.

34. Mark Noll, *The Scandal of the Evangelical Mind* (Grand Rapids, MI: Wm. B. Eerdmans Publishing Co., 1994), 51.

35. Herbert Schlossberg, *Idols for Destruction* (Nashville, TN: Thomas Nelson, 1983), 324.

36. Pratt, *Designed for Dignity*, 27.

37. Paul Stevens, *Doing God's Business: Meaning and Motivation* (Grand Rapids, MI: Wm. B. Eerdmans Publishing Co., 2006), 22.

38. James M. Renihan, "The Kingdom of God" <www.mountainretreatorg.net/eschatology/kingdom_god.html> (accessed May 1, 2010).

39. Graeme Goldsworthy, "The Kingdom of God and the Old Testament" <www.beginningwithmoses.org/articles/golds1.hhtm> (accessed May 1, 2010).

40. Miles Van Pelt, Biblical Theology, class lecture, Reformed Theological Seminary, Washington, DC, March 19, 2010.

41. Kevin DeYoung, "Thinking About the Kingdom" <www.thegospelcoalition.org/blogs/kevindeyoung/2009/10/07/thinking-about-kingdom> (accessed May 10, 2010).

42. George Ladd, *The Presence of The Future: The Eschatology of Biblical Realism* (Grand Rapids, MI: Wm. B. Eerdmans Publishing Co., 1974), 227.

43. Ladd, *Presence of The Future,* 227.

44. Oscar Cullman, *Christ and Time* (London: SCM Press, 1951), 84, 145-146.

45. Anthony Hoekema, *The Bible and the Future* (Grand Rapids, MI: Wm. B. Eerdmans Publishing Co., 1979), 29.

46. Cornelius Plantinga, *Engaging God's World: A Christian Vision of Faith, Learning, and Living* (Grand Rapids, MI: Wm. B. Eerdmans Publishing Co., 2002), 143.

47. Hoekema, *The Bible and the Future*, 45.

48. Hoekema, *The Bible and the Future*, 45.

49. Westminster Shorter Catechism, Question 102.

50. John Calvin, *Institutes of the Christian Religion, Volume 1* (Louisville, KY: Westminster John Koxx Press, 2006), 224.

51. Paul Marshall, *Heaven Is Not My Home: Learning to Live in God's Creation* (Nashville, TN: Thomas Nelson, 1998), 11.

52. Trevin Wax, Kingdom People Blog <trevinwax.wordpress. com/2008/06/16/the-growingkingdom-of-god> (accessed May 1, 2010).

53. Frame, "Is Natural Revelation Sufficient to Govern Culture," *Christian Culture* (Aug. 2006), 1-3.

54. Daniel Strange, "Co-belligerence and Common Grace: Can the enemy of my enemy be my friend?" *The Cambridge Papers,* Sept. 2005, vol. 14, no. 3.

55. Keller, *The Reason for God: Belief in an Age of Skepticism* (New York: Penguin Group, 2008), 53.

56. Herman Bavinck, *The Doctrine of God*, tr. William Hendriksen (Edinburgh: Banner of Truth, 1977), 208.

57. J.I. Packer, *Knowing God* (Downers Grove, IL: InterVarsity Press, 1993), 120.

58. John Murray, *Collected Writings of John Murray Volume 2: Lectures in Systematic Theology* (Edinburgh: Banner of Truth Trust, 1991), 93.

59. John Calvin, *Institutes of the Christian Religion*, 2.2.15.

60. Kuyper, *Encyclopedia of Sacred Theology* (New York: Charles Scribner's Sons, 1898), 279.

61. Murray, *Writings*, 96.

62. John Murray, "Common Grace," *Westminster Theological Journal,* 5, no. 1 (Nov. 1942): 28.

63. Westminster Confession of Faith, 16.7.

64. Tracey D. Lawrence, ed., *The Greatest Sermons Ever Preached* (Nashville, TN: Thomas Nelson, 2005), 98.

65. John Frame, *The Doctrine of God: A Theology of Lordship* (Phillipsburg, NJ: P&R Publishing, 2002), 431.

66. Murray, *Writings,* 102-103.

67. Murray, "Common Grace," 12.

68. John Frame, *The Doctrine of the Christian Life* (Phillipsburg, NJ: P&R Publishing, 2008), 860.

69. Wayne Grudem, *Bible Doctrine: Essential Teachings of the Christian Faith* (Grand Rapids, MI: Zondervan, 1999), 278.

70. Murray, *Writings,* 113.

71. Murray, *Writings,* 115.

72. Grudem, *Bible Doctrine,* 278.

73. Murray, "Common Grace," 25.

74. Murray, *Writings*, 117.

75. 75 Charles Colson and Nancy Pearcey, *How Now Shall We Live?* (Wheaton, IL: Tyndale House, 1999), xii.

76. Pearcey, *Total Truth*, 17.

77. Abraham Kuyper, *Abraham Kuyper: A Centennial Reader*, ed. James D. Bratt (Grand Rapids, MI: Wm. B. Eerdmans Publishing, 1998), 180.

78. John Calvin, *Institutes of the Christian Religion*, ed. John T. McNeill, tr. Ford Lewis Battles (Philadelphia, PA: Westminster Press, 1960), 75.

79. Francis Schaeffer, *Plan for Action: An Action Alternative Handbook for Whatever Happened to the Human Race?* (Old Tappan, NJ: Fleming H. Revell, 1980), 68.

80. Francis Schaeffer, *The Church at the End of the Twentieth Century,* in *The Complete Works of Francis A. Schaeffer,* Vol. 4 (Wheaton, IL: Crossway, 1982), 30.

81. Strange, "Co-belligerence and Common Grace."

82. R. Albert Mohler, Jr., "Standing Together, Standing Apart," *Touchstone,* July/August 2003, 17.

83. Scott Kauffmann, "The Problem of Good" <www.qideas. org/essays/the-problem-of-good.aspx> (accessed May 1, 2010).

84. Frame, *Doctrine of God,* 436.

85. Seth Godin, *The Dip: A Little Book That Teaches You When to Quit and When to Stick* (New York: Penguin Books, 2007), 4.

86. Tim Keller, *Counterfeit Gods: The Empty Promises of Money, Sex, and Power, and the Only Hope that Matters* (New York: Penguin Group, 2009), 75.

87. John Wooden, *My Personal Best: Life Lessons from an All-American Journey* (New York: McGraw-Hill, 2004), 90.

88. Spiros Zodhiates, *The Complete Word Study Dictionary: New Testament* (Chattanooga, TN: AMG Publishers, 1992), 507.

89. Warren W. Wiersbe, *The Bible Exposition Commentary: New Testament* (Wheaton, IL: Victor Books, 2003), Vol. 1, 92.

90. R.T. France, "Matthew," in *New Bible Commentary: 21st Century Edition,* 4th ed., ed. D. A. Carson, R.T. France, J.A. Motyer & G.J. Wenham (Downers Grove, IL: InterVarsity Press, 1994), 936-937.

91. Paul A. Marshall, *A Kind of Life Imposed on Man: Vocation and Social Order from Tyndale to Locke* (Toronto: University of Toronto Press, 1996), 25.

92. 92 Robert Banks and R. Paul Stevens, *The Complete Book of Everyday Christianity* (Downers Grove, IL: InterVarsity Press, 1997), 1000.

93. John Calvin, *The Epistles of Paul the Apostle to the Galatians, Ephesians, Philippians and Colossians* (Grand Rapids, MI: Wm. B. Eerdmans Publishing, 1996), 252.

94. Alister McGrath, "Calvin and the Christian Calling," *First Things,* June/July 1999, 94:34-35.

95. Marshall, *Kind of Life*, 26.

96. McGrath, "Calvin," 33.

97. Abraham Kuyper, *Calvinism: Six Lectures Delivered in the Theological Seminary at Princeton* (Bellingham, WA: Logos Research Systems, Inc., 2008), 25.

98. Kuyper, *Calvinism*, 25.

99. John Piper, "America's Debt to John Calvin," WORLD Magazine, July 4, 2009, vol. 24, no. 13.

100. Ben Chenoweth, "Identifying The Talents: Contextual Clues For The Interpretation Of The Parable Of The Talents," *Tyndale Bulletin,* 56.1 (2005), 65.

101. *The Oxford English Dictionary,* 2nd ed., Vol. 17 (Oxford: Clarendon, 1989), 580.

102. Craig L. Blomberg, *Interpreting the Parables* (Leicester: Apollos, 1990), 214.

103. Ivor Harold Jones, *The Matthean Parables: A Literary & Historical Commentary* (Leiden, Netherlands: Brill, 1995), 478.

104. Brad H. Young, *The Parables: Jewish Tradition and Christian Interpretation* (Peabody, MA: Hendrickson Publishers, 1998), 82.

105. John B. Carpenter, "The Parable of the Talents in Missionary Perspective: A Call for an Economic Spirituality," *Missiology,* 1997, 25:167.

106. Carpenter, "Parable," 168.

107. R. T. France, *Tyndale New Testament Commentary: Matthew* (Leicester: InterVarsity Press, 1985), 352.

108. John Paul Heil, "Final Parables in the Eschatological Discourse in Matthew 24-25" in Warren Carter & John Paul Heil, *Matthew's Parables: Audience-Oriented Perspectives* (Washington, DC: Catholic Biblical Association of America, 1998), 197.

109. Chenoweth, "Identifying the Talents," 61.

110. D. A. Carson, "Matthew," in *The Expositor's Bible Commentary*, ed. Frank E. Gaebelein, Vol. 8 (Grand Rapids, MI: Zondervan, 1984), 516.

111. Banks and Stevens, *Complete Book,* 1003.

112. F.D. Bruner, *Matthew: A Commentary—Volume 2: The Churchbook, Matthew 13-28* (Grand Rapids, MI: William B. Eerdmans Publishing Co., 2004), 551-162.

113. James Davison Hunter, *To Change the World: The Irony, Tragedy, and Possibility of Christianity in the Late Modern World* (New York: Oxford University Press, 2010), 93.

114. William Placher, ed., *Callings: Twenty Centuries of Christian Wisdom on Vocation* (Grand Rapids, MI: William B. Eerdmans Publishing Co., 2005), 262.

115. Gene Edward Veith, "Our Calling and God's Glory," *Modern Reformation,* Nov./Dec. 2007, vol. 16, no. 6, 22-28.

116. Plantinga, *Engaging,* 119.

117. Plantinga, *Engaging*, 120.

118. Blaise Pascal, *Pensees*, tr. A. J. Krailsheimer (New York: Penguin Classics, 1995), 57.

119. Chenoweth, "Identifying the Talents," 72.

Chapter 3: The History of Work and Calling

120. Aristotle, *Politics*, Book VIII, Chapter 2 (Charleston, SC: BiblioLife, 2006), 270.

121. Aristotle, *Nicomachean Ethics* (New York: Oxford University Press, 1925), 261.

122. W. A. Jurgens, "Letter to Diognetus," *Faith of the Early Fathers* (Collegeville, MN: Liturgical Press, 1970), 41.

123. Frame, "Christianity and Culture."

124. Eusedios of Caesarea, *Demonstration of the Gospel,* in *The Proof of the Gospel: Being the Demonstratio Evangelica of Eusebius of Caesarea,* vol. 1, tr. W.J. Ferrar (London: SPCK), 48-50.

125. Brian J. Walsh and Richard Middleton, *Transforming Vision: Shaping a Christian World View* (Downers Grove, IL: InterVarsity Press, 1984), 99.

126. Henlee H. Barnette, *Has God Called You?* (Nashville, TN: Broadman Press, 1965), 39-42.

127. Veith, *God at Work: Your Christian Vocation in All of Life* (Wheaton, IL: Crossway, 2002), 6.

128. Martin Luther, in *Selected Writings of Martin Luther,* ed. Theodore G. Tappert (Minneapolis, MN: Fortress Press, 2007), 430.

129. Lee Hardy, *The Fabric of This World: Inquiries into Calling, Career Choice, and the Design of Human Work* (Grand Rapids, MI: Wm. B. Eerdmans Publishing Co., 1990), 46.

130. Paul Althaus, *The Ethics of Martin Luther* (Philadelphia, PA: Fortress Press, 1972), 39-40.

131. McGrath, "Calvin," 31-35.

132. David Hall, Matthew Burton, *Calvin and Commerce: The Transforming Power of Calvinism in Market Economies* (Phillipsburg, NJ: P&R Publishing, 2009), 103-106.

133. Calvin, *Harmony of the Evangelists*, 2:143.

134. Christopher Elwood, *Calvin for Armchair Theologians* (Louisville, KY: Westminster John Knox Press, 2002), 160.

135. Crane Brinton, "Enlightenment," *Encyclopedia of Philosophy*, Vol. 2 (New York: Macmillan, 1967), 519.

136. Max Weber, *The Protestant Ethic and the Spirit of Capitalism: and Other Writings* (New York: Penguin Books, 2002), 1-202.

137. Alistair Mackenzie, *Faith and Work: From the Puritans to the Present*, Latimer Occasional Paper No 13 (Christchurch, New Zealand: Latimer Fellowship. March 2009), 9, <www.latimer.org.nz/downloads/faithandwork02.pdf> (accessed October 20, 2010).

138. Steve Garber, "Making Peace with Proximate Pustice (reprise)," *Comment*, February 15, 2008 <www.cardus.ca/comment/article/7> (accessed May 1, 2010).

Chapter 4. Our Current Situation

139. Gustaf Wingren, *Luther on Vocation* (Eugene, OR: Wipf & Stock Publishers, 2004), 9.

140. Laura Nash, Ken Blanchard and Scotty McLennan, *Church on Sunday, Work on Monday: The Challenge of*

Fusing Christian Values with Business Life (San Francisco: Jossey-Bass, 2001), 6.

141. Laura Nash, "Toward Integrating Work and Faith," *Religion and Liberty,* November-December 2002, vol. 12, no. 6, 2.

142. R. Paul Stevens, *The Other Six Days: Vocation, Work, and Ministry in Biblical Perspective* (Grand Rapids, MI: Wm. B. Eerdmans Publishing Co., 2000), 49.

143. Scott B. Rae, "Calling, Vocation, and Business," *Religion and Liberty,* November-December 2004, vol. 14, no. 6, Page 7.

144. Tim McConnell, "Vocation as Sustained Discipleship," *Praxis,* Summer 2010, 3.

145. Guinness, *The Call*, 31-32.

146. Guinness, *The Call*, 32.

147. Keller, *Counterfeit Gods*, xvii.

148. Keller, *Counterfeit Gods*, 171.

149. J. A. Donahue, "Careerism and the Ethics of Autonomy: A Theological Response," *Horizons,* vol. 15, no. 2 (1988), 318.

150. Schutt, *Redeeming Law*, 17.

151. Alan M. Webber, "Is Your Job Your Calling," Fast Company, January 31, 1998.

152. Veith, *God at Work,* 47.

153. 153 William Perkins, *The Work of William Perkins* (Appleford, England: Sutton Courtenay Press, 1969), 46.

154. 154 Keller, *Ministries of Mercy* (Phillipsburg, NJ: P&R Publishing, 1997), 112.

155. Alister McGrath, *Reformation Thought, An Introduction* (Malden, MA: Blackwell Publishing, 1999), 267

156. Sayers, *Creed*, 134-135

157. Martin Luther, *Luther's Works*, Vol. 5, Genesis Chapters 26-30 (St. Louis, MO: Concordia Publishing House, 1967), 102.

158. Perkins, "Treatise of the Vocations or Callings of Men," London, 1603. Reprinted in *The Work of William Perkins,* ed. Ian Breward (Appleford, England: Sutton Courtenay Press, 1970), 46.

159. Frederick Buechner, *Wishful Thinking: A Seeker's ABC* (San Francisco: Harper San Francisco, 1993), 119.

160. Roland H. Bainton, *Here I Stand: A Life of Martin Luther* (Nashville, TN: Abingdon, 1978), 180-81.

161. M. Kolden, "Luther on Vocation," *Word and World* 3, no. 4 (Fall 1983), 382-90.

162. Stevens, *Doing God's Business,* 22.

163. Lester DeKoster, *Work: The Meaning of Your Life* (Grand Rapids, MI: Christian's Library Press, 1982), 9.

164. John Stott, *Issues Facing Christians Today* (Basingstoke, England: Marshalls, 1984), 162.

165. Sayers, *Creed or Chaos?,* 89.

166. Veith, *God at Work,* 24.

167. Schaeffer, *A Christian Manifesto* (Wheaton, IL: Crossway, 1981), 17-18.

168. Wolters, *Creation Regained,* 60.

Chapter 5: The Future: Work, Calling, and Cultural Renewal

169. Keller, *What Is Christian Cultural Renewal?* (New York: MCM, 2003), 10.

170. Keller, "Work and Cultural Renewal" <www.faithandwork. org/workandculturalrenewal> (accessed May 1, 2010).

171. Thomas Cahill, *How the Irish Saved Civilization* (New York: Random House, 1995), 145ff.

172. Bill Crouse, "The Church and Culture: The Need for a New Mind," *Reformation & Revival,* Summer 1994, 63.

173. "Barna Survey Examines Changes in Worldview Among Christians Over the Past 13 Years" <www.barna.org/barna-update/article/12-faithspirituality/252-barna-survey-examines-changes-inworldviewamong-christians-over-the-past-13> (accessed May 1, 2010).

174. Dietrich Bonhoeffer, *Meditations on the Cross* (Louisville, KY: Westminster John Knox Press, 1998), 61.

175. Dietrich Bonhoeffer, *The Cost of Discipleship*, tr. R. H. Fuller (New York: The Macmillan Company, 1963), 99.

176. McGrath, *A Life of John Calvin: A Study in the Shaping of Western Culture* (Oxford, England: Basil Blackwell Ltd., 1990), 184.

177. Barrett Gritters, "Calvin as Model for Reformed Ministers," *Protestant Reformed Theological Journal*, vol. 43, no. 1., Nov. 2009, 18.

178. Douglas Wilson, *The Case for Classical Christian Education* (Wheaton, IL: Crossway, 2003), 96.

179. Walsh and Middleton, *Transforming Vision,* 69.

180. Collin Hansen, "Young, Restless, Reformed," *Christianity Today*, September, 2006, 32 <www.christianitytoday.com/ct/2006/009/42.32.html> (Accessed May 1, 2010).

181. John Calvin, *Institutes of the Christian Religion,* ed. John T. McNeill, Vol. 1 (Louisville, KY: Westminster John Knox Press, 1973), 690.

182. J. Ligon Duncan, "A Call to Give Yourself to God," sermon preached Jan. 23, 2002 at The First Presbyterian Church, Jackson, MS<www.fpcjackson.org/resources/sermons/

romans/romansvol5to6/38aRomans.htm> (accessed May 1, 2010).

183. Plantinga, *Not the Way It's Supposed to Be* (Grand Rapids, MI: Wm. B. Eerdmans Publishing Co., 1995), 10.

184. Scott Kauffman, "The Problem Of Good" <www.qideas.org/essays/the-problem-of-good.aspx> (accessed May 20, 2010).

185. David Dark, *Everyday Apocalypse* (Grand Rapids, MI: Brazos Press, 2002), 18.

186. Nicholas Wolterstorff <www.calvin.edu/about/shalom.htm> (accessed May 15, 2010).

187. Henry Blackaby, *Experiencing God* (Nashville, TN: Broadman & Holman, 2004), 69.

188. Gabe Lyons, "Cultural Influence: An Opportunity for the Church," *Comment,* March 2008, <www.cardus.ca/comment/article/1550>.

189. Herman Bavinck, "The Origin, Essence, and Purpose of Man," *Reformed Perspectives Magazine,* vol. 9, no. 25, June 17-23, 2007.

190. Tim Keller, "A New Kind of Urban Christian," *Christianity Today,* vol. 50, no. 5, May 2006.

191. H. Richard Niebuhr, *Christ and Culture* (New York: Harper Collins, 1951), 45-218.

192. Donald G. Bloesch, *Freedom for Obedience* (San Francisco: Harper & Row, 1987), 227.

193. Bloesch, *Freedom,* 227.

194. Bloesch, *Freedom,* 227.

195. Whitney Hopler, "Use Your Creativity to Change the Culture" <www.crosswalk.com/spirituallife/11573937/page0/> (accessed May 1, 2010).

196. Hunter, *To Change the World,* 45.

197. James Hunter, "Faithful Presence," interview by Christopher Benson, *Christianity Today,* vol. 54, May 2010.

198. Hunter, *To Change the World,* 89.

199. Rodney Stark, *The Rise of Christianity* (Princeton, NJ: Princeton University Press, 1996), 161.

200. D. James Kennedy and Jerry Newcombe, *What If Jesus Had Never Been Born?* (Nashville, TN: Thomas Nelson, 1997), 1-9.

201. John Frame, *The Doctrine of the Christian Life* (Phillipsburg, NJ: P&R Publishing, 2008), 943.

202. Alvin Schmidt, *How Christianity Changed the World* (Grand Rapids, MI: Zondervan, 2004), 12.

203. Pearcey, *Total Truth,* 18.

204. T.M. Moore, "Work, Beauty, and Meaning: A Biblical Perspective on the Daily Grind," October 06, 2006 <www.justicefellowship.org/features-columns/archive/1571-work-beauty-and-meaning> (accessed May 1, 2010).

205. James Hunter, "To Change the World," *The Trinity Forum Briefing* (McLean, VA: The Trinity Forum, 2002), vol. 3, no. 2, 10-11.

206. Tim Keller and James Hunter, *Getting Upstream to Transform the City* (New York: Redeemer Church Planting Center, 2003), 15.

207. 207 Bloesch, *Freedom,* 54.

208. Tim Keller, *Ministry in the New Global Culture of Major City-Centers* (NY: Redeemer Presbyterian Church, 2008), 16.

209. 209 Gabe Lyons, "Influencing Culture" <www.qideas.org/essays/influencing-culture.aspx> (accessed May 1, 2010).

210. Richard Doster, "The Kingdom Work of the Corporate World," *By Faith,* no. 11, October 2006.

211. John Frame, *The Doctrine of the Christian Life* (Phillipsburg, NJ: P&R Publishing, 2008), 944.

212. Hunter, *To Change the World,* 45.

213. Lyons, "Influencing Culture."

Chapter 6: Conclusion: How Then Shall We Work?

214. Richard Leider and David Shapiro, *Repacking Your Bags: Lighten Your Load for the Rest of Your Life* (San Francisco: Berrett-Koehler Publishers, 2002), 33.

215. David Bornstein, *How to Change the World: Social Entrepreneurs and the Power of New Ideas* (NY: Oxford University Press USA, 2007), 1-10.

216. Douglas Groothuis, *Truth Decay: Defending Christianity Against the Challenges of Postmodernism* (Downers Grove, IL: InterVarsity Press, 2000), 269.

217. Frame, *Doctrine of the Christian Life,* 861-862.

218. Groothuis, *Truth Decay,* 279.

219. Geerhardus Vos, *The Shorter Writings of Geerhardus Vos*, ed. Richard B. Gaffin, Jr., (Phillipsburg, NJ: P&R Publishing, 1980), 260-261.

220. William Edgar, "Geerhardus Vos and Culture," in *Resurrection and Eschatology: Theology in Service of the Church, Essays in Honor of Richard B. Gaffin Jr.,* ed. L. Tipton and J. Waddington (Phillipsburg, NJ: P&R Publishing, 2008), 393.

221. Tim Keller, "The Gospel in All its Forms," *Christianity Today International/Leadership Journal.* Spring 2008, vol. XXIX, no. 2, 16.

222. Keller, "Gospel in All its Forms," 16.

223. Plantinga, *Engaging God's World,* xii.

224. Groothuis, *Truth Decay,* 270.

225. Mark D. Roberts, "Let It Flow Out: An Interview with N. T. Wright" <blog.beliefnet.com/markdroberts/nt wright/2009/01/index.html#ixzz1GNyOuh6L> (accessed May 1, 2010).

226. Paul Marshall, *Heaven is Not My Home: Learning to Live in God's Creation* (Nashville, TN: Word Publishing, 1998), 243.

227. Dane W. Fowlkes, *Kingdom Campus: Re-envisioning the Christian College as a Kingdom Resource,* Paper, Council of Christian Colleges and Universities, Washington, D.C., July 30, 2003.

228. Calvin, *Commentary on the Harmony of the Gospels*, Luke 10:38.

229. Lyons, "Influencing Culture," www.qideas.org/essays/ influencing-culture.aspx (accessed May 1, 2010).

230. Moore, "Work, Beauty, and Meaning."

231. Hermann Hagedorn, *Sunward I've Climbed: The Story of John Magee, Poet and Soldier 1922-1941 (New York: The Macmillan Company, 1944), 165.*

232. Mark Driscoll and Gerry Breshears, *Doctrine: What Christians Should Believe* (Wheaton, IL: Crossway, 2010), 411.

233. McGrath, "Calvin," 31-35.

Further Reading

Colson, Charles and Nancy Pearcey. *How Now Shall We Live*. Wheaton, IL: Tyndale House, 1999.

Guinness, Os. *The Call: Finding and Fulfilling the Central Purpose of Your Life*. Nashville, TN: Word Publishing, 1998.

Plantinga, Cornelius. *Engaging God's World: A Christian Vision of Faith, Learning, and Living* Grand Rapids, MI: Eerdmans, 2002.

Pratt, Richard L. *Designed for Dignity: What God Has Made it Possible for You to Be*. Phillipsburg: Presbyterian and Reformed Publishing, 1993.

Duzer, Jeff Van. *Why Business Matters to God: And What Still Needs to Be Fixed*. Downers Grove, IL: InterVarsity Press, 2010.

Kuyper, Abraham. *Wisdom & Wonder: Common Grace in Science & Art*. Grand Rapids: Christian's Library Press, 2011.

Sherman, Amy. *Kingdom Calling: Vocational Stewardship for the Common Good*. Downers Grove, IL: InterVarsity Press, 2011.

Wright, Christopher J. H. *The Mission of God: Unlocking the Bible's Grand Narrative*. Downers Grove, IL: InterVarsity Press, 2016.

38328846R00098

Made in the USA
Lexington, KY
03 January 2015